Book
Cover
Designs

Book

Cover

   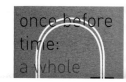

Designs

Matthew Goodman

Foreword by Nicole Caputo

Schiffer
Publishing Ltd

DEDICATION

To Bill Jones: a mentor and friend.
Thank you for giving me
the opportunity to do what I love.

ACKNOWLEDGMENTS

I would like to thank and acknowledge all the designers who participated in the creation of this book, for without your submissions and hard work this collection would not have been possible. Special thanks also to the publishers and publishing companies for allowing the designers to showcase their work for the good of the publishing and design community.

Copyright © 2016 by Matthew Goodman

Library of Congress Control Number: 2015952539

InDesign and PhotoShop are registered trademarks
Day-Glow is a registered trademark

Type set in Didot & Proxima Nova

ISBN: 978-0-7643-5016-0

Printed in China

Published by Schiffer Publishing, Ltd.
4880 Lower Valley Road
Atglen, PA 19310
Phone: (610) 593-1777; Fax: (610) 593-2002
E-mail: Info@schifferbooks.com

For our complete selection of fine books on this and related subjects, please visit our website at www.schifferbooks.com. You may also write for a free catalog.

This book may be purchased from the publisher.
Please try your bookstore first.

We are always looking for people to write books on new and related subjects. If you have an idea for a book, please contact us at proposals@schifferbooks.com.

Schiffer Publishing's titles are available at special discounts for bulk purchases for sales promotions or premiums. Special editions, including personalized covers, corporate imprints, and excerpts can be created in large quantities for special needs. For more information, contact the publisher.

CONTENTS

FOREWORD

*The Future of the Cover Designer
in the Digital Age*

by Nicole Caputo

When Matthew first contacted me to write the foreword for this book, I was honored. But when he told me the topic—The Future of the Cover Designer in the Digital Age—I hesitated. I hesitated because I don't know exactly what the future holds. What I do know is that I am tremendously grateful to be a designer of books and their covers at what feels like an increasingly exciting moment, when design has never been more important.

My design career began in the midst of gloomy predictions about how the rise of digital media would mean the fall of the printed book. For many people, the question was not "if" but "when." Fortunately, however, these predictions about the death of the printed book have proven to be greatly exaggerated. Now, at the beginning of my second decade as a designer, there's no mistaking the fact that print books are more appreciated, more noticed, more treasured—and more carefully designed and displayed—than ever before.

Printed books remain an important part of the publishing business. This is especially clear in the categories of serious non-fiction, which sell over the long term in backlists and offer ample opportunities for repackaging. Imprints, such as Vintage, continue to breathe new life into literary classics through brilliant design. Most publishers have learned from experience that only twenty percent of their annual sales in these categories tend to be in e-format. And they have also learned the design of books in these categories has never mattered more. New eye-catching techniques continue to emerge, as designers have used the need to justify the relatively high price point of the print versus the e-version as an opportunity for experimentation and innovation. And even though the cover approval process may now invite more careful scrutiny, due in part to a difficult selling climate in which there are increasingly fewer things publishers can control, I think this heightened scrutiny too reflects the recognition that cover and book design are an ever-more integral part of the reading and book-buying experience.

Far from fearing the end of print, we as designers can thank the emergence of e-books for making it easier to persuade clients of the advantages of new treatments, some of which would have previously been considered too lavish. Lenticular printing techniques, 3D printing, stamped cases and paper over boards, foil inks and uncoated stock are just a few of the many possibilities that I have enjoyed in recent years or admired in the work of others. In short, it seems that the easy availability and low cost of e-books has encouraged us to re-imagine the print book as a unique, irresistible, even artisanal object. If these hand-held artifacts are perhaps most loved by the indie stores, this too is a happy development since the indie stores are experiencing new influence as vibrant sources of growth for many publishers, capable of transforming a sleeper into a blockbuster through passionate, old-fashioned hand-selling.

Perhaps the greatest cause for optimism is the way literary fiction and serious non-fiction are no longer the only categories that feature brilliant design. Cookbooks, for example, now often skip the kitchen entirely and head straight to the coffee table, where their visually enthralling, artfully photographed full-color images make them perfect companions for art and other luxuriously illustrated books.

Even the categories that have done especially well in e-form—commercial best-seller fiction, business, romance, erotica and self-help—are beginning to show a notable design-consciousness. It used to be the case that the relatively short lifespan of these categories was reflected in their formulaic covers. With their generic and vague typographic solutions and large, full-bleed image selections beneath garish, faux-embossed typography, these books seemed to be designed mainly to show that they were just like all the other books in the category—maybe not identical, but close enough. For example, with upwards of sixty percent of their sales in electronic data, the categories of romance and erotica were viewed as quick reads, digested swiftly on a plane or train and rarely consulted again. Quite unlike writerly titles such as Lily King's historical novel *Euphoria* or Thor Hanson's lyrical natural science book, *The Triumph of Seeds*; these e-friendly books were not designed as intimate objects that readers would want to keep close by, to remind themselves and others of who we are.

But now, even these once-formulaic categories are beginning to sparkle. The need to design for e-tail outlets has inspired several design trends, including "flat design," where simple elements are easier to make work across multiple environments. Illustrations take on a more minimalist, icon-like appearance comprised of basic shapes with clean, smooth lines and edges filled with bright, bold color, all composed within a frame that features plentiful breathing space. Beyond readability on screen, it seems to me that this cleaner approach is gaining popularity due to a need to declutter days in which we are relentlessly bombarded by information from multiple devices. Flat design brings a form of quiet, not only to screens, but to the analog world of print as well.

As a designer who believes that books are a vital part of our culture, I feel a certain sense of mission. I am not just responsible for creating a concept and an image that will entice and provoke a viewer to want to purchase a book at first glance, but also for making a beloved object that people will want to hold in their hands and display on their tables and shelves. We are creating a heightened idea of reading—an experience. I feel a sense of pride when I see the vibrant array of choices available across so many different categories each time I walk into any one of the bookstores that are beginning to reappear all of over New York City. These design-savvy objects appeal to us in wildly different ways: Some of them flirt from the shelf, others shout from the screen and—some through my personal favorite method of book seduction—beg to be picked up from the tables, touched, and maybe even sniffed.

Nicole's work can be viewed on pages 174-177

PREFACE

To understand why this book came about, I first need to explain where I began in my profession.

In the Fall of 2000, I had just graduated from the Art Institute of Philadelphia and was anxious to start my career. After months of searching and applying to different design jobs, I landed my first position at an independent book publisher, Running Press.

I worked for Running Press for nearly a decade, designing a wide variety of books and packages. While there, I looked for different books to gain inspiration, but couldn't seem to find one suitable for showcasing work for the publishing industry at that time.

This brings me to today. Working as a freelance designer and an in-house designer for Schiffer Publishing, I saw an opportunity to design the book I've always envisioned. With some research and help from many professionals in the industry today, that book is finally here.

—

When creating this book, I knew that I would need to contact each designer individually to gather information about their careers, along with a small portfolio of covers to showcase their work. Being a designer myself, I was interested in knowing how each designer went about creating their covers, so I asked each designer to write a brief description of their creative process. I felt other professionals in any design medium could benefit from this knowledge and apply it to their daily practices. I also felt that students currently pursuing their design studies would profit from the knowledge provided and would also gain a perspective on what a career in the design profession might be like. But choosing designers from such a vast and varied industry was difficult—I needed a list, and their were a few things I looked for when starting.

I began with designers who inspired me. Working in the publishing industry myself, I wanted to design a book that I would pick up and be excited by, as well as to provide a great sampling that would benefit the design community as a whole. Next, I wanted the designers to have a range in experience. I didn't want to showcase only designers with twenty years of experience who had, over their careers, won multiple awards—and their are plenty of designers in this book with that kind of resume—but I also wanted to showcase designers who were just starting out in the industry. I personally believe that knowledge and perception change with the experience one gains when working in any profession. The more experience gained, the better the work becomes. So with this in mind, you will see that each designer from the design veteran and to the ones just starting out—and those in between, the category

I fall into—has his or her own point of view and unique process/style that tends to work when activating and maintaining the design principles learned both in school and on the job.

I then looked to the most important aspect of this collection: the individual designer. Throughout this project, every single designer I had the pleasure to speak to or interact with showed passion and dedication for their craft. With the amount of talent each designer possessed, it was truly comforting to see how humble each was. The amount of hard work and professionalism each designer had was evident in the work they supplied to me. I was truly inspired...and I, too, was humbled. (I can't say enough good things about each individual in this book!)

Finally, I wanted the work to be current. I wanted to showcase the industry as it is today, including the trends, ranging from font choices to hand-drawn typography, to photographic and illustration styles, and other design characteristics, so that years from now, this reference would provide a great overview of what was happening in the publishing industry in the early 2000s. Even though the principles and practices remain the same, styles come and go and are inspired and started by the working professionals in the industry. Many people, including me, look forward to and are inspired by the boundaries people continue to push with design in the publishing industry.

My hope is that no matter if you are a student, a professional, or just interested in book design, you will find this collection a useful and inspiring reference. I hope you enjoy the book!

All the Best,
Matt Goodman

THE DESIGNERS

Adam Johnson

Adam Johnson is a designer and illustrator who has worked in publishing since 2007. Originally from near Syracuse, New York, he received his bachelor degree from Brigham Young University, in Provo, Utah. Adam enjoys exploring dusty libraries, throwing dance parties, and eating waffles. He lives in California with his wife and four children.

The Designer's Approach: I begin a project with research to understand the book's competitive landscape, the readership, and mood or feel of the story; I'll usually collect images as I do this. Sometimes I'll read some of the manuscript to get a sense of the writing style, or I may just get a description of the story and key themes, or details from the editor. Next, I try to establish a concept through word lists, sketches, and thumbnails. Then I'll begin to put pieces together, continue to flesh out photo research, and select or create type that builds on the concept and tone. Once these elements come together, I'll refine them, present them, and revise accordingly.

Pg 14, all covers: Harper Perennial | Pg 15, top left: Harper Perennial; top right: Harper Perennial; bottom left: Harper Perennial; bottom right: It Books | Pg 16, top left: Harper Perennial; top right: William Morrow; bottom left: Harper Voyager; bottom right: Harper Perennial | Pg 17, top left: HarperCollins Publishers; top right: William Morrow; bottom: William Morrow

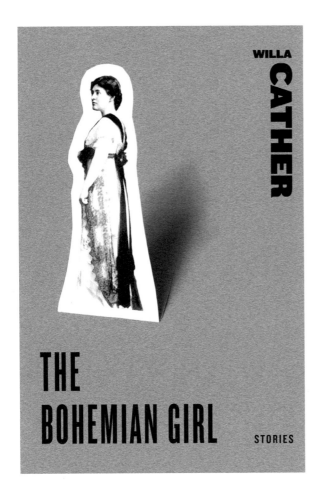

WILLA **CATHER**

THE BOHEMIAN GIRL

STORIES

FYODOR **DOSTOYEVSKY**

A DISGRACEFUL AFFAIR

STORIES

HERMAN **MELVILLE**

THE HAPPY FAILURE

STORIES

LEO **TOLSTOY**

FAMILY HAPPINESS

STORIES

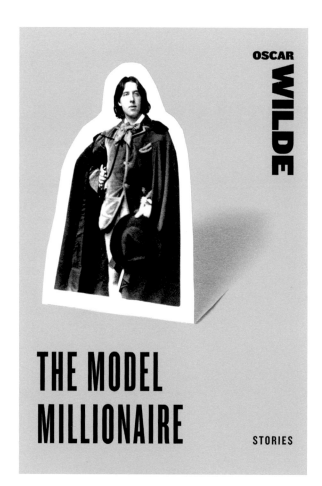

OSCAR **WILDE**

THE MODEL MILLIONAIRE

STORIES

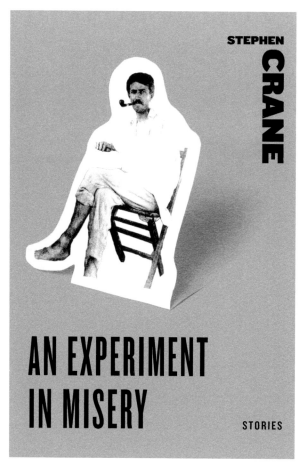

STEPHEN **CRANE**

AN EXPERIMENT IN MISERY

STORIES

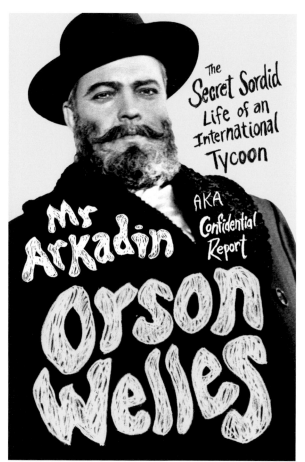

The Secret Sordid Life of an International Tycoon

Mr Arkadin

AKA Confidential Report

Orson Welles

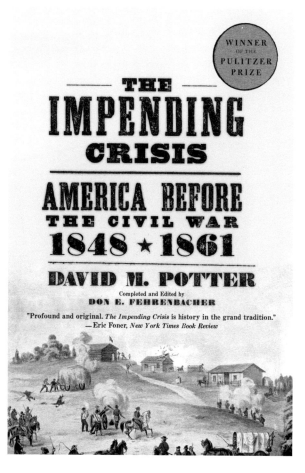

WINNER OF THE PULITZER PRIZE

THE IMPENDING CRISIS

AMERICA BEFORE THE CIVIL WAR 1848 ★ 1861

DAVID M. POTTER

Completed and Edited by
DON E. FEHRENBACHER

"Profound and original. *The Impending Crisis* is history in the grand tradition."
—Eric Foner, *New York Times Book Review*

BRADBURY *the martian chronicles*

HARPER**PERENNIAL** • MODERN**CLASSICS**

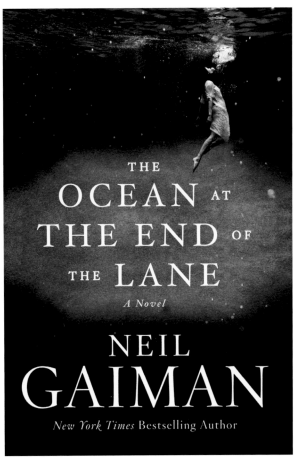

THE OCEAN AT THE END OF THE LANE

A Novel

NEIL GAIMAN

New York Times Bestselling Author

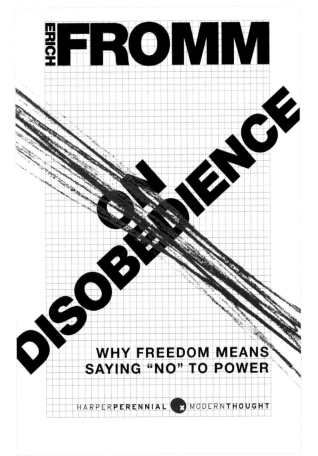

ERICH FROMM

ON DISOBEDIENCE

WHY FREEDOM MEANS SAYING "NO" TO POWER

HARPER**PERENNIAL** • MODERN**THOUGHT**

"Powerful . . . Brimming with philosophical conundrums . . . Cargill's world is abundant in detail and imagery in the service of the story. . . . Will keep readers entranced." —*PUBLISHERS WEEKLY* (starred review)

A NOVEL

QUEEN OF THE DARK THINGS

C. ROBERT CARGILL

The Acclaimed Author of *Dreams and Shadows*

"AN ELEGANT AND COMPLEX THRILLER. . . . INGENIOUS. . . .
HARROWINGLY BEAUTIFUL." —NEW YORK TIMES BOOK REVIEW

THE
redbreast

AUTHOR OF *NEMESIS*
JO NESBØ

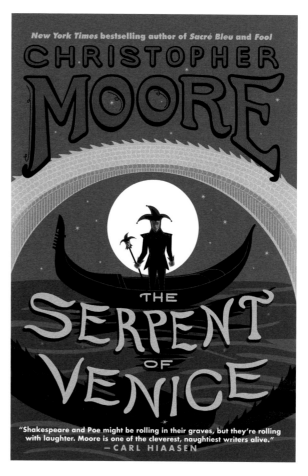

New York Times bestselling author of *Sacré Bleu* and *Fool*
CHRISTOPHER MOORE

THE
SERPENT
OF
VENICE

"Shakespeare and Poe might be rolling in their graves, but they're rolling
with laughter. Moore is one of the cleverest, naughtiest writers alive."
—CARL HIAASEN

NEW YORK TIMES BESTSELLER
A NOVEL BY ELMORE LEONARD

"*Swag* hits dead center . . . captures a slice of
urban life better than anything else I've read."
—DETROIT FREE PRESS

$wag

Adly Elewa

Adly Elewa has been designing book covers professionally since his graduation from the School of Visual Arts. A born-and-bred New Yorker, Adly has spent time in the design departments of noted publishing giants Farrar, Straus and Giroux and Penguin Random House. He currently runs his own studio, and has a diverse portfolio of memorable fiction and nonfiction covers under his belt.

The Designer's Approach: I'm constantly thinking about design, whether I'm at my desk at Penguin or in the crowd at a punk show on the weekends. I've found inspiration in sources as diverse as a friend's fashion designs, the 8-bit video games of my childhood, protest posters of the 1960s, and new wave music, among other references bouncing around in my brain. I also rely heavily on my personal tumblr to collect all sorts of still image and video references that reflect specific textures, patterns, and color palates that could match the mood of whichever title I happen to be conceptualizing.

I've had to switch often between fiction and nonfiction titles, and each demands a different process. With fiction, it's obviously more important to read the manuscript as soon as I can get my hands on it and apply my initial thematic impressions to a mood board. I'll always consider the stylistic ephemera of the novel, the author's voice, and the generic conventions it plays with to conceive an image that's both striking and textually relevant. Nonfiction necessitates a more direct approach, similar to that of an editorial illustration, with a clever graphic summary of the book's argument or idea. I always like to picture the targeted reader of each particular title and try to echo their interests and peculiarities, which ultimately leads to a much richer portfolio that isn't bogged down by my own stylistic crutches. The ultimate goal with every cover is to identify an image that sticks with the reader, while also reaching a happy compromise between publisher, author, and designer.

Pg 19, top left: Penguin Press; top right: Penguin Press; bottom left: Farrar Straus and Giroux, Design: Rodrigo Corral Art—Adly Elewa; bottom right: Farrar Straus and Giroux, Cover Design: Adly Elewa and Rodrigo Corral | Pg 20, top left: Farrar Straus and Giroux; top right: Penguin Books; bottom left: Overlook Press; bottom right: Melville | Pg 21, left: New Directions; right: Farrar Straus and Giroux

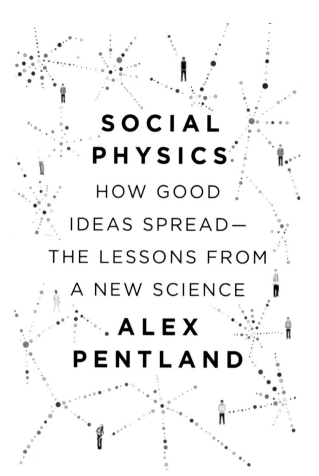

SOCIAL
PHYSICS
HOW GOOD
IDEAS SPREAD—
THE LESSONS FROM
A NEW SCIENCE
ALEX
PENTLAND

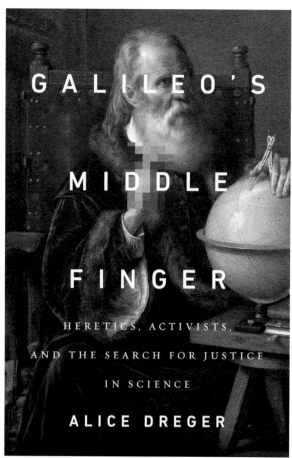

GALILEO'S
MIDDLE
FINGER
HERETICS, ACTIVISTS,
AND THE SEARCH FOR JUSTICE
IN SCIENCE
ALICE DREGER

Reinventing Bach
Paul Elie

A Novel
The
Marriage
Plot
Jeffrey
Eugenides
Winner of the
Pulitzer Prize

THE
WISDOM OF
PSYCHOPATHS
WHAT SAINTS, SPIES, AND
SERIAL KILLERS CAN TEACH
US ABOUT SUCCESS
KEVIN DUTTON

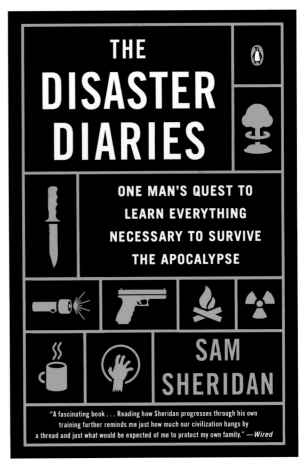

THE
DISASTER
DIARIES

ONE MAN'S QUEST TO
LEARN EVERYTHING
NECESSARY TO SURVIVE
THE APOCALYPSE

SAM
SHERIDAN

"A fascinating book . . . Reading how Sheridan progresses through his own
training further reminds me just how much our civilization hangs by
a thread and just what would be expected of me to protect my own family." —Wired

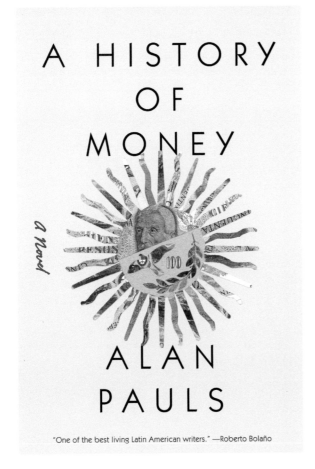

A HISTORY
OF
MONEY

A Novel

ALAN
PAULS

"One of the best living Latin American writers." —Roberto Bolaño

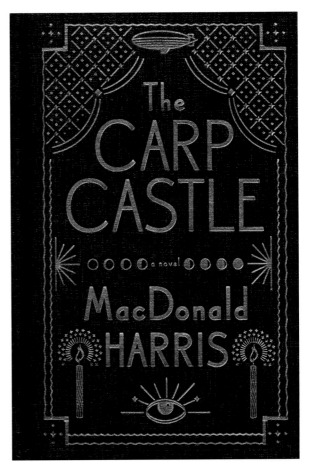

The
CARP
CASTLE
a novel
MacDonald
HARRIS

LIGHTNING RODS

RODS

HELEN DE WITT

Author of THE LAST SAMURAI

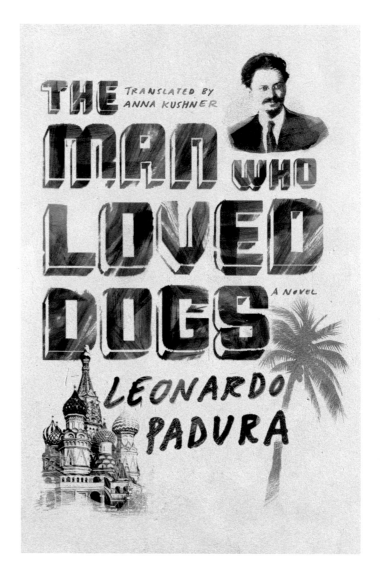

THE MAN WHO LOVED DOGS

TRANSLATED BY ANNA KUSHNER

A NOVEL

LEONARDO PADURA

Alex Merto

Alex Merto is a designer living and working in New York. He is co-owner of a multi-disciplinary studio in Brooklyn called Graphiatrist. Alex has worked at multiple publishing companies, including Penguin Random House and Farrar, Straus and Giroux.

The Designer's Approach: My process begins with reading the manuscript. I like to give myself enough time to be able to read it, but also be able to separate myself from it. Most of my ideas come when I'm doing something else, not completely focusing on the project or trying to find a solution. Throughout the process, I take a lot of notes and scribble down a lot of words or images that I think best represent the mood or purpose of the book. I try a lot of ideas . . . even some that I know won't be the final solution, but might help lead me to something else. In the end, I narrow the ideas down until I feel like I've got something that really works and that will stand out on a bookshelf.

Pg 23, **top left:** Mulholland Books; **top right:** Mulholland Books; **bottom left:** Blue Rider Press; **bottom right:** Farrar, Straus and Giroux | Pg 24, **left:** Riverhead Books; **right:** Random House | Pg 25, **top left:** Plume; **top right:** Riverhead Books; **bottom left:** Riverhead Books; **bottom right:** Penguin Books

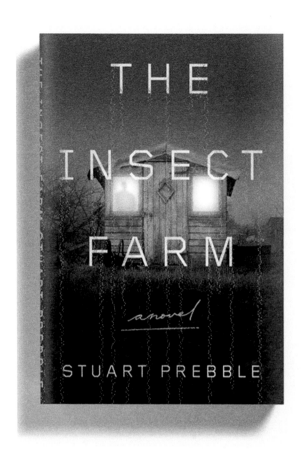

THE INSECT FARM

a novel

STUART PREBBLE

WRITTEN IN THE BLOOD

A NOVEL

STEPHEN LLOYD JONES

FIFTY MICE

DANIEL PYNE

A NOVEL

NEAR AND DISTANT NEIGHBORS

A NEW HISTORY OF SOVIET INTELLIGENCE

JONATHAN HASLAM

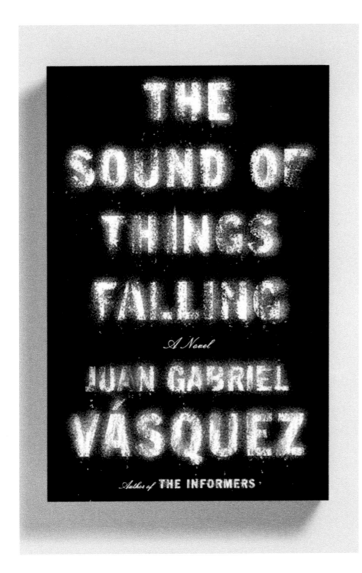

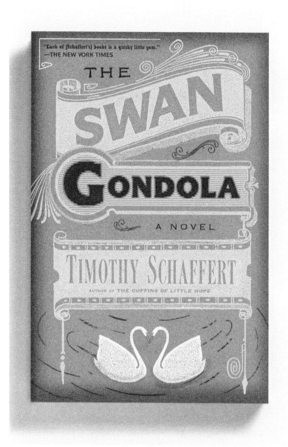

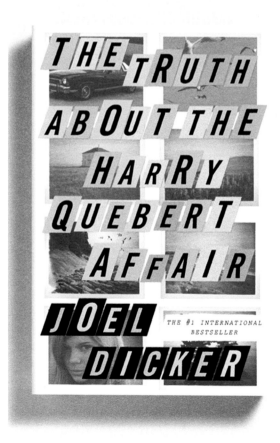

Alex Camlin

Alex Camlin is the creative director at *Da Capo Press* for the Perseus Books Group in Boston, where he has designed and art directed covers and jackets for various imprints over the past fifteen years. He is also the designer for *Harvard Review*, and creates book covers and interiors for several other publishers. Aside from books and their covers, his work includes posters, magazine covers, logos, and editorial illustration—and a website. Alex has taught courses in book design at Emerson College, lectured on cover design for various classes and panels, and is a member of The Society of Printers. His award-winning designs have been honored by the AIGA's "50 Books/50 Covers" competition, *Print* magazine's "Regional Design Annual," AIGA Boston, the New York Book Show, and Bookbuilders of Boston.

The Designer's Approach: I generally describe my work as being graphic: built less on photography and "painterly" imagery, and more on letterform, line art, primary color, and geometric form. Contrasts create meaning, and I tend to rely on strong differences in scale, weight, color, texture, and shape to achieve meaningful juxtapositions. Some combination of geometric and organic forms are often the result. If there is a single "style" or common quality to be found in my work, it probably owes something to my belief in Modernism, love of typography, and mid-century design.

Pg 27, top left: Da Capo Press; top right: Columbia University Press, Art Director: Julia Kushnirsky; bottom left: Jacket for David Mamet; bottom right: Mariner Books, Art Director: Christopher Moisan I Pg 28, top left: Harvard Review 45; top right: Da Capo Press; bottom left: Harvard Review 41; bottom right: Da Capo Press I Pg 29, left: Picador, Art Director: Henry Sene Yee; right: Da Capo Press

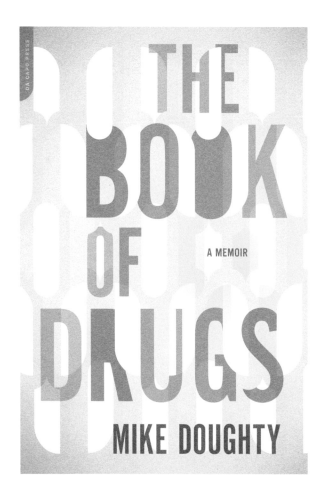

THE
BOOK
OF
DRUGS

A MEMOIR

MIKE DOUGHTY

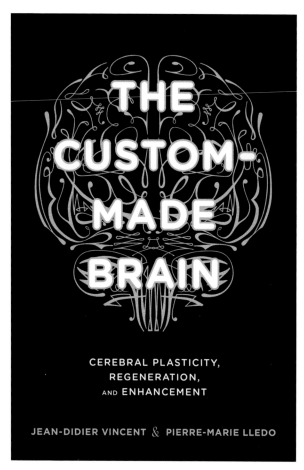

THE
CUSTOM-
MADE
BRAIN

CEREBRAL PLASTICITY,
REGENERATION,
AND ENHANCEMENT

JEAN-DIDIER VINCENT & PIERRE-MARIE LLEDO

DAVID MAMET

WAR
3
STORIES

NOVELLAS

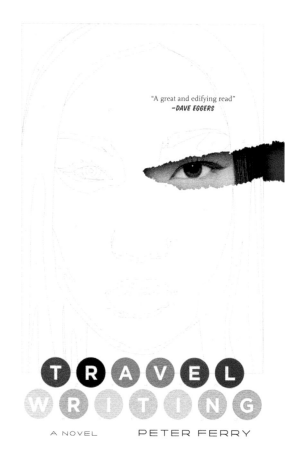

"A great and edifying read"
—DAVE EGGERS

TRAVEL
WRITING

A NOVEL   PETER FERRY

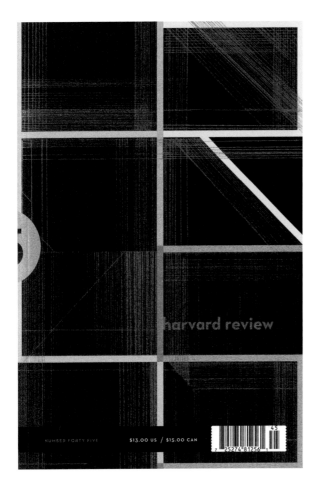

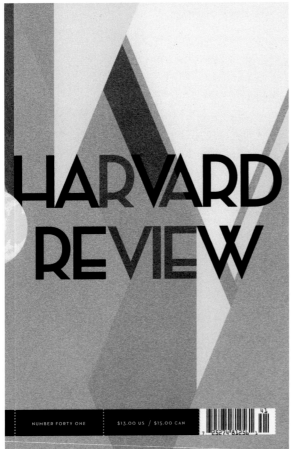

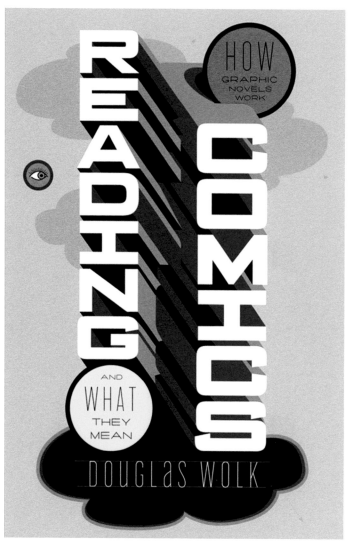

Bill Jones

Bill Jones has been designing book covers freelance since 2013, but was the design director of Running Press for over fifteen years prior. Before that, he successfully directed Cowles Creative Publishing (now known as Creative Publishing International) as their executive vice president/creative director, for nearly twenty years.

The Designer's Approach: I spent my earlier years in the business doing consumer product packaging design, advertising, and new product concept development. Book design became my focus later on as our company's business evolved in that direction.

Package design was an outstanding training ground for book cover design as both are the primary consumer interface for the product. However, consumer product packaging presents a much simpler challenge than book cover design. The package designer needs to differentiate a product from a relative few competitors on the shelf, competitors that have a known look. Also, product packages are nearly always displayed face out.

Book cover design presents a much greater challenge in two ways. First, your cover is competing for consumer attention with not just a few competitors, but with hundreds or even thousands. Secondly, books are, more often than not, displayed spine out rather than face out providing the designer with a much smaller display area to attract a buyer's attention.

At times, the greatest design challenges can come from within the publishing company. Editors and sales people often have an idea how a book of a certain category should look and, at the same time, want the cover to stand out from others in the same category. "Be different, but not too different."

Since most of my cover design has been for nonfiction books, I look for solutions that combine a clear statement of the product's benefits with a graphic treatment that is arresting and evokes something positive about the book. To start, I try to gain an understanding of the target audience—age, gender, education level, etc.—and then look for graphic ideas that will appeal to that demographic.

Pg 31, all covers: Running Press | Pg 32, all covers: Running Press

ROAM THE GLOBE

DELAYING
THE REAL
WORLD

Make
The World
A Better
Place

BY COLLEEN KINDER

A TWENTYSOMETHING'S
GUIDE TO SEEKING
ADVENTURE

FIND A
COOL JOB

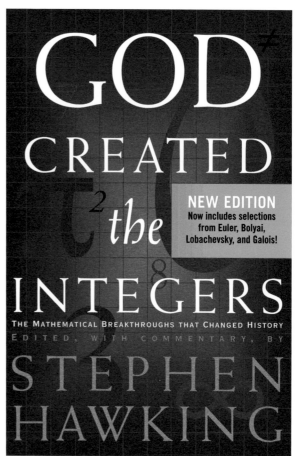

GOD ≠
CREATED
²the

NEW EDITION
Now includes selections
from Euler, Bolyai,
Lobachevsky, and Galois!

INTEGERS

THE MATHEMATICAL BREAKTHROUGHS THAT CHANGED HISTORY

EDITED, WITH COMMENTARY, BY

STEPHEN
HAWKING

porn·ol·o·gy

noun—1: A Good Girl's Guide to Porn;
2: The misadventures of the world's first
anthro*PORN*ologist; 3: A Hilarious
Exploration of Men, Relationships, and Sex.

Ayn Carrillo-Gailey

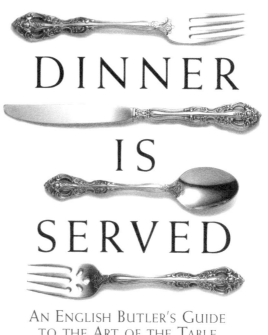

DINNER
IS
SERVED

AN ENGLISH BUTLER'S GUIDE
TO THE ART OF THE TABLE

BY ARTHUR INCH
TECHNICAL ADVISOR FOR THE FILM *GOSFORD PARK*
AND
ARLENE HIRST
SENIOR EDITOR, *METROPOLITAN HOME*

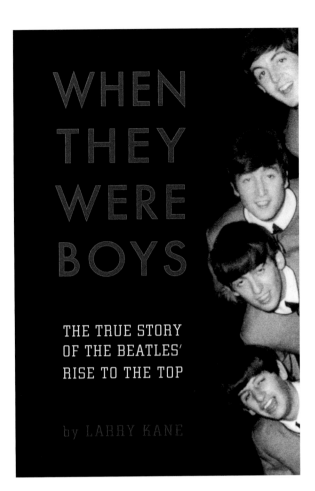

WHEN
THEY
WERE
BOYS

THE TRUE STORY
OF THE BEATLES'
RISE TO THE TOP

by LARRY KANE

"An engaging and inspiring guide for everyone who wants to drink well and think big."
—Daniel Pink, author of A Whole New Mind

WINE
DRINKING
for
INSPIRED
THINKING

Uncork
Your
Creative
Juices

"HIGHLY
RECOMMENDED."
—Robert M. Parker Jr.

Michael J. Gelb
Author of the international bestseller, How to Think Like Leonardo Da Vinci

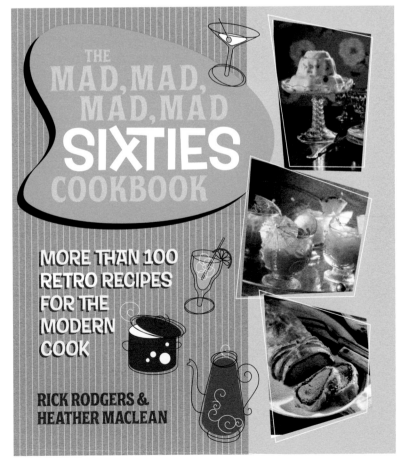

THE
MAD, MAD,
MAD, MAD
SIXTIES
COOKBOOK

MORE THAN 100
RETRO RECIPES
FOR THE
MODERN
COOK

RICK RODGERS &
HEATHER MACLEAN

Catherine Casalino

Catherine Casalino is an award-winning art director and designer based in New York City. Catherine began her career at Rodrigo Corral Design and has worked in-house at Simon & Schuster, Random House, and Grand Central Publishing, where she oversaw the Twelve list. She is currently a Senior Art Director at Regan Arts. She also freelances for publishing houses and other clients throughout the US and abroad. Her design work has been recognized by AIGA, *Print* magazine, the Type Directors Club, *Communication Arts*, *Eye* magazine, and the New York Book Show.

The Designer's Approach: When I'm designing a book cover, I always try to approach it as a completely unique project. Where sometimes as an artist it's advantageous to have a style, as a designer and art director, I really try to avoid having a style or falling back on techniques I used on past jobs—no matter how bestselling or award-winning the book was.

Each book that comes across my desk is unique and I want to make sure to package them as such. The jobs I work on range widely from novels to current events to celebrity books, so I really get the chance to stretch in all directions and problem solve in new ways.

I spend a lot of time collecting. I bookmark artists I like. I buy art books constantly. I'm always squirreling away stuff that might be useful on some future project. The satisfaction that comes with matching up the perfect concept, photographer, or image with a book is the same no matter the budget, the time it takes to solve the problem, or the technique. Some days I am art directing photo shoots with a dozen people on set, and some days it's just me and a pencil.

Pg 34, top left: Twelve Books, Illustration: Marc Burckhardt; top right: Grand Central Publishing; bottom left: Grand Central Publishing; bottom right: Grand Central Publishing, Photography: Melanie Dunea, Illustration: Ross MacDonald Publishing I Pg 35, top: Simon & Schuster; bottom left: Twelve Books; bottom right: Grand Central Publishing I Pg 36, left: Simon & Schuster; right: Grand Central Publishing, Photography: Ryann Cooley

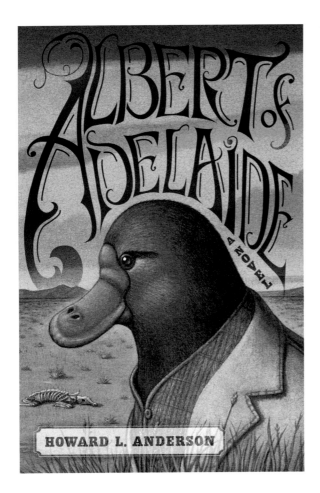

FICTION

A DELIGHTFUL AND TERRIFYING COLLECTION OF TWENTY
SHORT STORIES, EDITED BY CRITICALLY ACCLAIMED WRITER
AND NOVELIST MARK JUDE POIRIER.

ADOLESCENCE. Fortunately it's over with early, and once you've
finished paying for the therapy, there's still a chance to move on
with your life.

THE WORST YEARS OF YOUR LIFE says it all: angst, depression,
growing pains, puberty, nasty boys and nastier girls; these are
stories of awkwardness and embarrassment from a stellar list of
contributors. Great postmodern classics like John Barth's "Lost in the
Funhouse" are paired with newer selections, such as Stacey Richter's
"The Beauty Treatment" and A.M. Homes's "A Real Doll," in this
searing, unforgettable collection. A perfect book for revisiting old
favorites and discovering new ones, and the opportunity to relive the
worst years of your life — without having to relive the worst years
of your life.

MARK JUDE POIRIER (editor) is a novelist and screenwriter.
He is the author of the novels MODERN RANCH LIVING and
GOATS, and the story collections UNSUNG HEROES OF
AMERICAN INDUSTRY and NAKED PUEBLO.

© DIANA OSSANA

Cover design and illustration by Catherine Casalino
Register online at www.simonsays.com
for more information on this and
other great books.

Simon +
Schuster
Paperbacks

U.S. $15.00/Can. $18.99

08071500

ISBN-13: 978-1-4165-4926-0
ISBN-10: 1-4165-4926-9

51500

9 781416 549260

Simon +
Schuster
Paperbacks

THE WORST YEARS OF YOUR LIFE

Mark
Jude
Poirier,
editor

Edited by Mark Jude Poirier

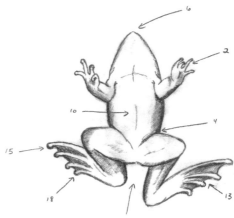

The **WORST** Years
of Your Life

Stories for the Geeked-Out, Angst-Ridden, Lust-Addled,
and Deeply Misunderstood Adolescent in All of Us

1. George Saunders
2. Jennifer Egan
3. Victor D. LaValle
4. Julie Orringer
5. John Barth
6. Rattawut Lapcharoensap
7. Stanley Elkin
8. Stacey Richter
9. Jim Shepard
10. Alicia Erian
11. A.M. Homes
12. Robert Boswell
13. Kevin Canty
14. Mark Jude Poirier
15. Amber Dermont
16. Nathan Englander
17. Malinda McCollum
18. Chris Adrian
19. Elizabeth Stuckey-French
20. Holiday Reinhorn

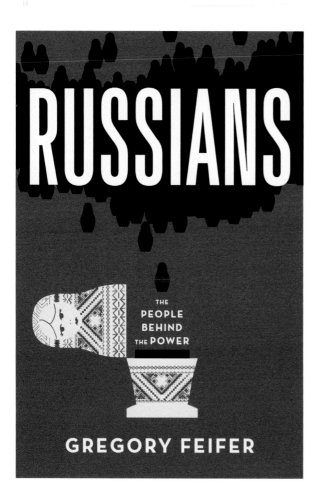

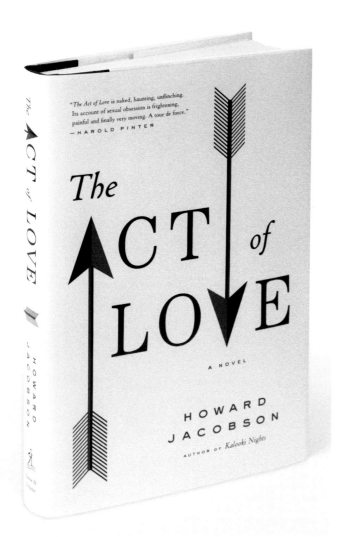

Charlotte Strick

For fourteen years **Charlotte Strick** was a designer and art director for Faber & Faber Inc. and the paperback line at Farrar, Straus and Giroux. Her work has been featured in the AIGA "50 Books/50 Covers" show, the TDC Annual Exhibition, *Print* magazine, the Book Binder's Guild Annual Awards Show, and many books about cover design. The proud owner of a coveted Silver Cube from The Art Directors Club, Charlotte is also designer and art editor of the distinguished *Paris Review* magazine. Her writings on art and design have been published by *The Paris Review*, *The Atlantic,* and *The Huffington Post*. In 2014, she partnered with Claire Williams Martinez to form Strick&Williams, a boutique, multidisciplinary design firm focused on the arts, education, publishing, non-profits, and everything in-between. A graduate of Parsons School of Design, Charlotte lives in Brooklyn, New York, with her husband, their twin boys, and a giant bowl of goldfish.

The Designer's Approach: Whenever possible I start with the text. It's what's *in* the book that is going to lead me to each original solution. A jacket designer works very much like a detective in this way— searching for the scenes, or even the sentences, that sum up a book and set it apart. This is especially true of fiction. With non-fiction, your hunt may be through the archives of historical institutions or museums. The author likely has invaluable research to share from many years of study, and when you have only a few short weeks to read and conceptualize a cover design, this is a real gift.

I keep a small note pad near me when I'm reading a manuscript. I'm often reading multiple books at a time, and I name each page or pages, by the title and author, and then I write all my ideas (both interesting and obvious) on the pages. I often copy down passages and page numbers, too, to jog memories and remember the voice of a character or the tone of the author. I have piles of these notebooks at this point. They also include deadlines and feedback from editors, authors, and art directors, along with the names of illustrators or photographers whose work I think would marry well with the writing. If I'm art directing the title, I'll include other designers' names, too.

Pg 37: Courtesy of Stephanie de Rouge | Pg 38, top left: Farrar, Straus & Giroux, Art Director: Rodrigo Corral; top right: Faber and Faber, Illustrator: Ariana Nehmad Ross; bottom left: Farrar, Straus & Giroux, Art Director: Rodrigo Corral; bottom right: Farrar, Straus & Giroux, Art Director: Rodrigo Corral | Pg 39: Farrar, Straus & Giroux, Book 1: *Jupiter and Semele*, Gustave Moreau, Book 2: *Academy*, Cy Twombly, Book 3: *Sea Sponges from Albertus Seba's Cabinet of Natural Curiosities*, Art Director: Susan Mitchell | Pg 40, top left: Farrar, Straus & Giroux; top right: Farrar, Straus & Giroux Originals, Illustrator: Eric Nyquist; bottom left: Farrar, Straus & Giroux; bottom right: Farrar, Straus & Giroux Originals | Pg 41, top left: Straus & Giroux / Farrar, Straus & Giroux Originals, Illustrator: Patrick Leger; top right: Farrar, Straus & Giroux, Art Director: Rodrigo Corral; bottom left: Straus & Giroux / Farrar, Straus & Giroux Classics, Illustrator: Lindsay Meyer-Beug; bottom right: Farrar, Straus & Giroux, Illustrator: Chris Silas Neal, Art Director: Susan Mitchell

. . . because, they said, she was lazy. What they meant by lazy was that she used too many contractions: for instance, she would not write out in full the words cannot and will not, but instead contracted them to **can't and won't**.

(stories)

Lydia Davis.

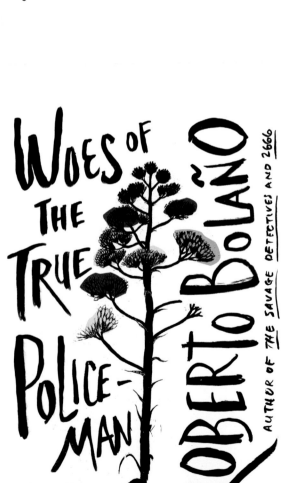

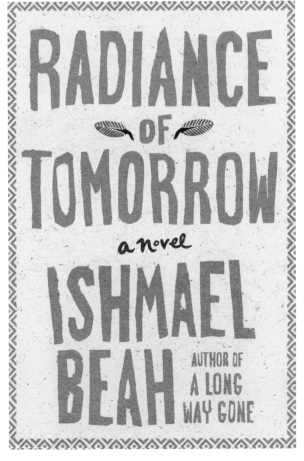

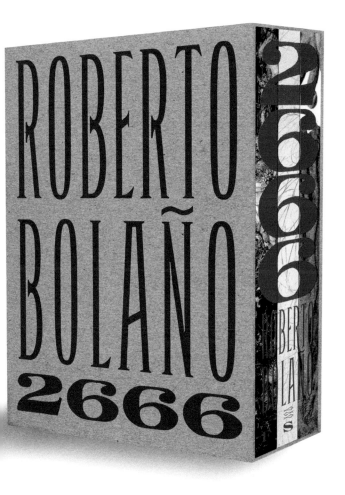

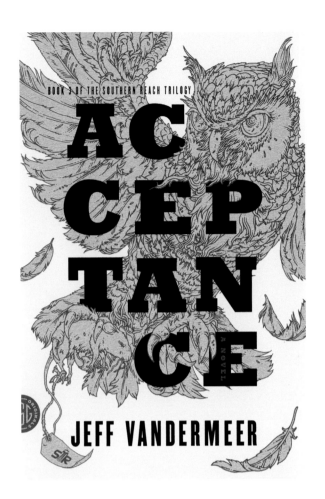

BOOK 3 OF THE SOUTHERN REACH TRILOGY

ACCEPTANCE

A NOVEL

JEFF VANDERMEER

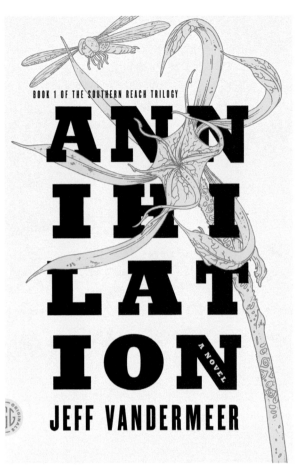

BOOK 1 OF THE SOUTHERN REACH TRILOGY

ANNIHILATION

A NOVEL

JEFF VANDERMEER

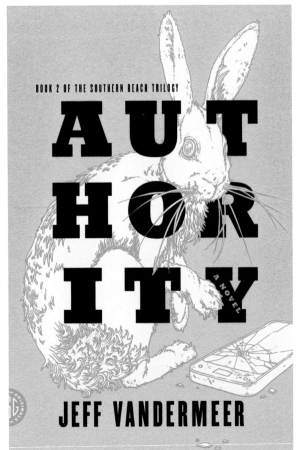

BOOK 2 OF THE SOUTHERN REACH TRILOGY

AUTHORITY

A NOVEL

JEFF VANDERMEER

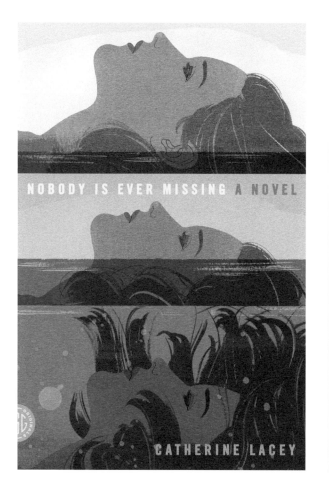

NOBODY IS EVER MISSING A NOVEL

CATHERINE LACEY

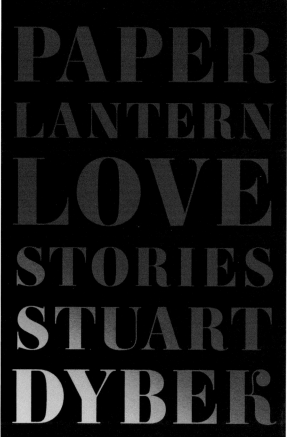

PAPER LANTERN LOVE STORIES STUART DYBEK

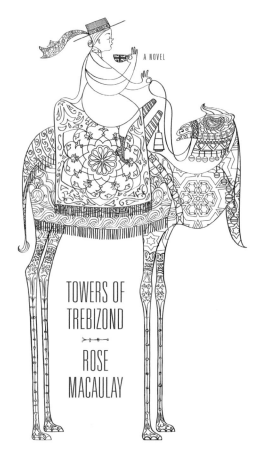

A NOVEL

TOWERS OF TREBIZOND

ROSE MACAULAY

Poser

my life in
twenty-three
yoga poses
Claire Dederer

Chelsea Hunter

Chelsea Hunter received her BFA in graphic and interactive communications from Ringling College of Art and Design in 2011, with a minor in business of art and design. She is currently a designer at Basic Books, where she has worked since 2012 designing politics, history, science, and economics book covers.

The Designer's Approach: Most of the cover designs that I work on are often linked with specific subjects and moments in history, and the cover should help the reader recall those time periods. Finding and using the appropriate historic image requires careful research of both the source material and the available images. Often, these images cannot be manipulated in any way, which makes it both challenging and exciting as a designer to come up with creative solutions that integrate the image into the cover design in a way that is pleasing, while remaining respectful of the image or original artwork.

Pg 43, all covers: Basic Books, Art Director: Nicole Caputo I Pg 44, left: Basic Books, unpublished design, Art Director: Nicole Caputo; right: Basic Books, Art Director: Nicole Caputo

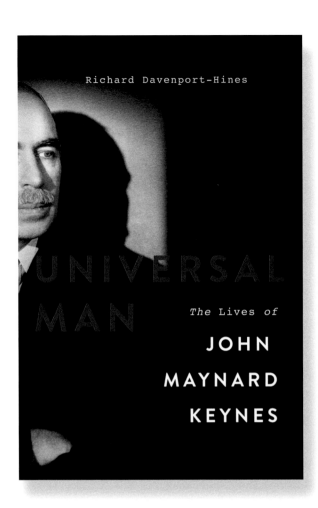

Richard Davenport-Hines

UNIVERSAL
MAN

The Lives *of*
**JOHN
MAYNARD
KEYNES**

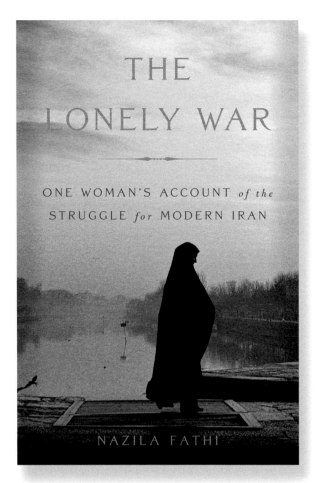

THE
LONELY WAR

ONE WOMAN'S ACCOUNT *of the*
STRUGGLE *for* MODERN IRAN

NAZILA FATHI

Christopher Hitchens

"Hitchens exhibits
precisely the combination of
indignation and intellect that
he recommends to others."
—*New York Times
Book Review*

LETTERS TO A YOUNG
CONTRARIAN

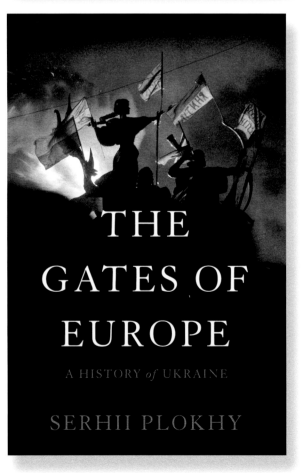

THE
GATES OF
EUROPE

A HISTORY *of* UKRAINE

SERHII PLOKHY

DESTRUCTION
WAS MY BEATRICE

Dada

and the

Unmaking

of the

Twentieth

Century

JED RASULA

"A magnificent book, an honor to its writer... a book that
makes for a return of civilized discussion of the question
of the morality of war."—*New York Review of Books*

JUST
AND
UNJUST
WARS

A MORAL ARGUMENT
WITH HISTORICAL ILLUSTRATIONS
Fifth Edition

MICHAEL WALZER
With a New Preface and Postscript by the Author

Christopher Moisan

Christopher Moisan is creative director of Mariner, the trade paperback imprint of Houghton Mifflin Harcourt, where he oversees a wide range of projects including graphic books and the covers of the *Best American* series. He also does freelance work for a variety of clients. His designs have been featured in AIGA's "50 Books/50 Covers," the *Print Regional Design Annual*, *How* magazine, AIGA Best of New England, Bookbuilders of Boston, and *The Book Cover Archive*. Previously, he worked as a book conservator and as a designer at WGBH | PBS in Boston. He holds a BFA in graphic design from Rhode Island School of Design and lives in Brooklyn, New York.

The Designer's Approach: The first question I'm usually asked when people discover I design book covers is whether I read the books before working on them. The answer is always emphatically "Yes!" Each book is in its own language and creates its own world, and the ability to draw upon my research and interests to design appropriately and individually is my favorite aspect of my job. I might be working on a novel set in Victorian England one day and short stories set in Nigeria in the 1990s the next—and then, the following day, into the twenty-second century with a science fiction book. Recently, cover design has moved in a more illustrative direction and that's given me an opportunity to pick up a brush and pen and exercise a lot of creativity.

Pg 46, top left: Mariner; top right: Mariner; bottom left: Mariner; bottom right: Houghton Mifflin Harcourt | Pg 47, top left: Mariner Original; top right: Houghton Mifflin Harcourt; bottom left: Mariner; bottom right: The New Press | Pg 48, left: Mariner Original; right: Mariner Original

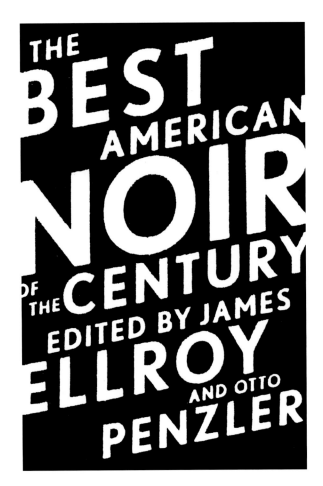

"Precise, exhilarating, sometimes wonderfully funny and always beautiful."
— MARGOT LIVESEY, author of *The House on Fortune Street*

THE
ARCHITECT
OF
FLOWERS
STORIES
BY
WILLIAM
LYCHACK

still
LIFE

ADVENTURES
IN
TAXIDERMY

MELISSA MILGROM

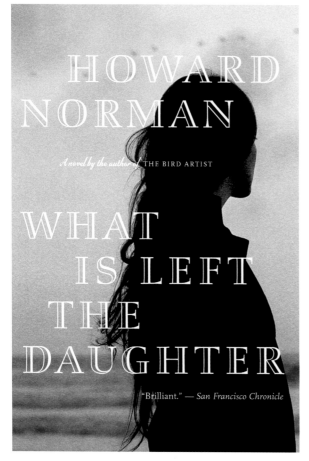

HOWARD
NORMAN

A novel by the author of THE BIRD ARTIST

WHAT
IS LEFT
THE
DAUGHTER

"Brilliant." — *San Francisco Chronicle*

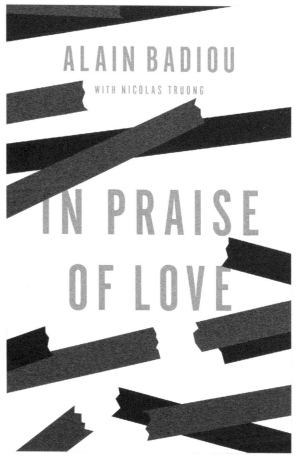

ALAIN BADIOU
WITH NICOLAS TRUONG

IN PRAISE
OF LOVE

Christopher Sergio

Christopher Sergio is an award-winning art director at Penguin Random House with over a decade of book cover design and art direction experience. In addition to his publishing work, he is the principal of Christopher Sergio Design, whose work includes design for clients in film, media, and the arts, and illustration for clients such as *The New York Times*. Chris is a graduate of the Rhode Island School of Design, Fiorello H. LaGuardia High School of Music & Art and Performing Arts, and is a native New Yorker.

The Designer's Approach: The book itself is your client and best guide while designing. As a designer and art director, I always look to the manuscript or central idea of the book for my inspiration. Making a direct connection with the material is an essential first step to creating a great book cover design. It ensures that you're drawing water from the deepest well.

Almost all of my work is conceptually driven, so my design process always starts with ideas—good, bad, and ugly! As I read and respond to the manuscript, I'll usually jot down or thumbnail-sketch any ideas that aren't blatant duds, although sometimes it's helpful to even get a few bad ideas down on the page. Once I come up with several ideas that feel right, I'll dive in and start making.

One of the best parts about designing covers is the imperative I set to constantly re-educate myself and learn new techniques as part of my design process. So, for instance, on *Alif the Unseen*, after I had the ambitious idea to create a calligraphic logo that suggested Arabic script for the main character "ALIF," that meant doing lots of primary source research, followed by hours and hours of drawing and refining the logo, both by hand and on the computer, until the final result felt both plausibly "Arabic" and graphically resolved.

In this same way, I've learned aspects of studio photography, become an expert on German blackletter typography (temporary), created original Zen ink-brush paintings called Enso, become a maven of women's fashion (extremely temporary), and illustrated an art deco cruise ship poster—all in the service of cover concepts I conceived of, but wasn't initially sure I could pull off.

The life of a book cover designer and art director is one of exhilarating, daunting, never-boring experimentation, and self-improvement. It's fun as hell.

Pg 50, top left: Portfolio/Penguin, Cover photo: Gabrielle Revere; top right: Grove/Atlantic; bottom left: Self-initiated; bottom right: Farrar, Straus & Giroux | Pg 51, left: Random House; right: HarperCollins | Pg 52, top left: Spiegel & Grau; top right: Galleri Riis, Oslo, Norway, Cover and interior book design of monograph for the Norwegian-American artist Håvard Homstvedt. Cover is foil stamped over cloth.; bottom left: Henry Holt; bottom right: Gallery Books / Simon & Schuster

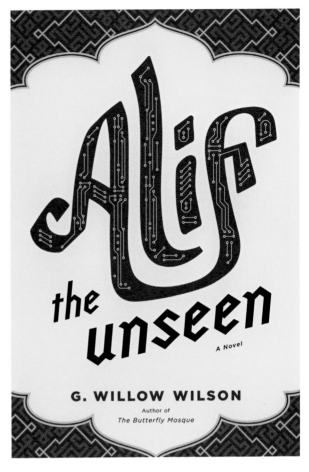

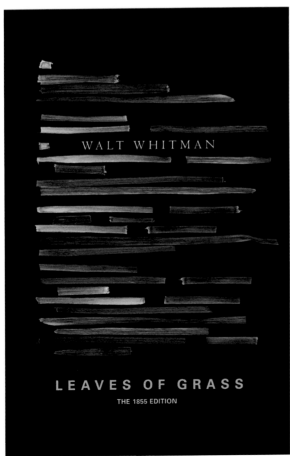

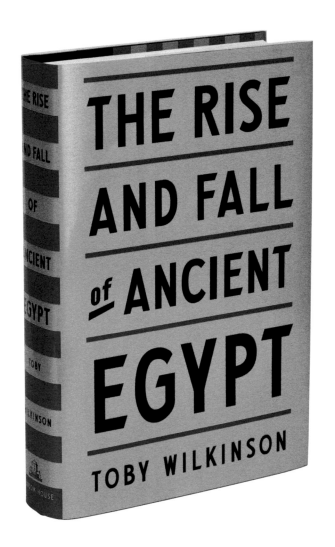

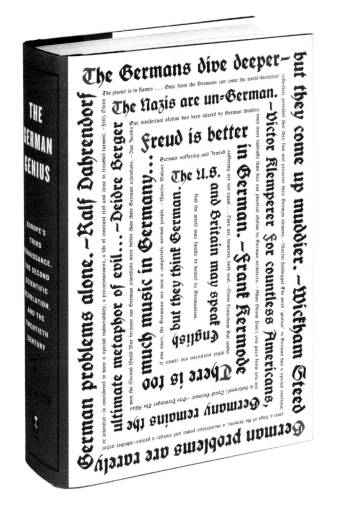

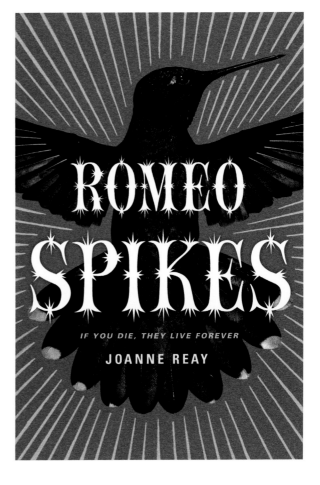

Connie Gabbert

After spending her freshman year of college at the School of the Museum of Fine Art in Boston studying drawing and painting, **Connie Gabbert** transferred back home to the West Coast. She completed her BFA at Cornish College of the Arts in Seattle, where she studied illustration and design.

After graduating, Faceout Studio (in central Oregon) gave Connie her dream job: designing book covers. There, she met her husband, also a cover designer. After working at the studio for about a year and a half, she left to stay home with her first baby girl.

However, Connie soon found herself missing cover design, and that led her to start her own business. She's been freelancing ever since, and she indicates that it's very hard to imagine a better job. She is privileged to work with some amazing people on inspiring projects—while still being able to spend much of her time with her family.

The Designer's Approach: As far as my process goes, it seems to vary from cover to cover. Each book has it's own unique voice, subject matter, and audience, and I try to approach each title with a consideration for what suits it best. Sometimes that means I can put together a looser composition, with hand-drawn type and fun border. Other times a more serious, linear layout with a classic typeface is more appropriate. That's one of the amazing things about designing covers: every project is different. Every day at work poses a different challenge than the last.

I definitely enjoy bringing my illustration background into cover design, both through typography and imagery. I recently added a Wacom Cintiq to my studio, which has allowed me to draw directly onto my covers without having to touch a scanner.

Pg 54, top left: Open Road Media, Art director: Andrea Worthington; top right: Atria, Art director: Jeanne Lee; bottom left: Thomas Nelson, Art director: Julie Allen/Belinda Bass; bottom right: Georgetown University Press, Art director: Deborah Weiner I Pg 55, top left: Harper Collins, Art Director: Jeanne Reina, Photograph by Tiffany Lausen; top right: Atria, Art Director: Jeanne Reina; bottom left: Atria, Art director: Jeanne Lee; bottom right: Thomas Nelson, Art Director: Kristen Ingebretson I Pg 56, top left: Oxford University Press, Art Director: Brady McNamara; top right: Thomas Nelson, Art director: Kristen Vasgaard; bottom left: Houghton Mifflin Harcourt, Art director: Rebecca Bond/Scott Magoon; bottom right: Algonquin, Art director: Anne Winslow/Elise Howard

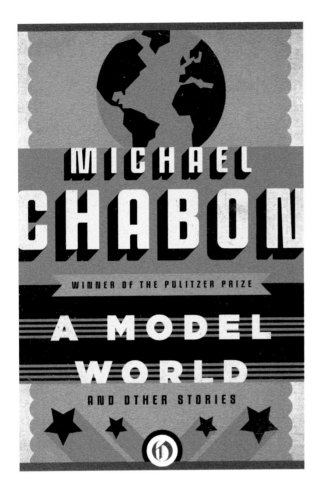

MICHAEL CHABON

WINNER OF THE PULITZER PRIZE

A MODEL WORLD

AND OTHER STORIES

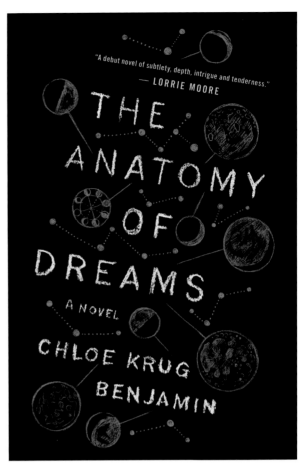

"A debut novel of subtlety, depth, intrigue and tenderness."
— LORRIE MOORE

THE ANATOMY OF DREAMS

A NOVEL

CHLOE KRUG BENJAMIN

NOTES FROM A

Blue Bike

The Art of Living Intentionally in a Chaotic World

TSH OXENREIDER

Founder of TheArtofSimple.net

FOREWORD BY ANN VOSKAMP,
New York Times best-selling author of
One Thousand Gifts

CHINA'S SENT-DOWN GENERATION

PUBLIC ADMINISTRATION AND THE
LEGACIES OF MAO'S RUSTICATION PROGRAM

HELENA RENE

A NOVEL *of*
DINING *and* DECEIT

food WHORE

jessica tom

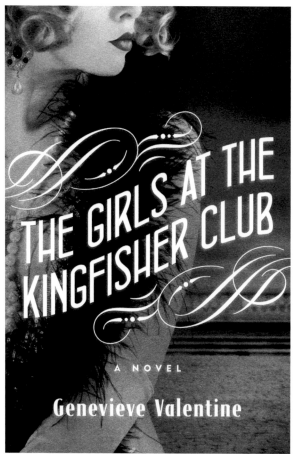

THE GIRLS AT THE KINGFISHER CLUB

A NOVEL

Genevieve Valentine

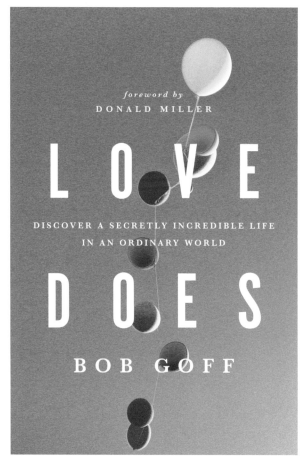

foreword by
DONALD MILLER

L O V E

DISCOVER A SECRETLY INCREDIBLE LIFE
IN AN ORDINARY WORLD

D O E S

BOB GOFF

Eat Play Sleep

the ESSENTIAL guide
to Your BABY'S FIRST 3 MONTHS
Luiza DeSouza

Coming Up Short

WORKING-CLASS ADULTHOOD IN AN AGE OF UNCERTAINTY

Jennifer M. Silva

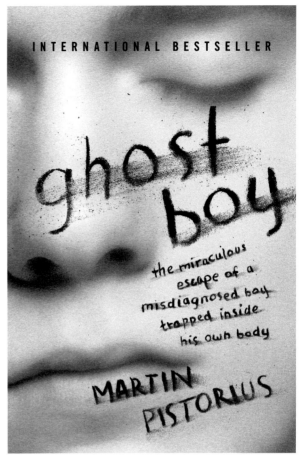

INTERNATIONAL BESTSELLER

ghost boy

the miraculous escape of a misdiagnosed boy trapped inside his own body

MARTIN PISTORIUS

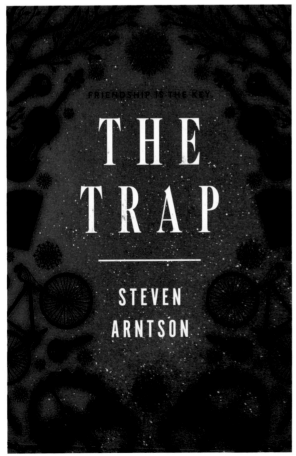

FRIENDSHIP IS THE KEY.

THE TRAP

STEVEN ARNTSON

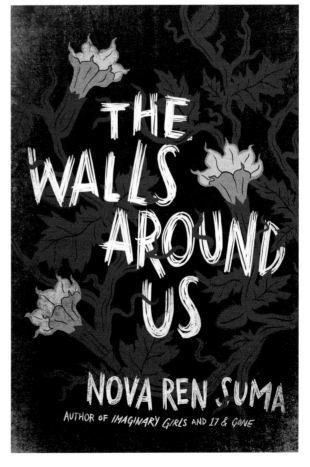

THE WALLS AROUND US

NOVA REN SUMA

AUTHOR OF IMAGINARY GIRLS AND 17 & GONE

Crush Creative is a truly integrated design agency providing creative solutions across all print, digital, and moving media since 1998. Having worked for all the major publishing companies, Crush specializes in book cover design for the fiction market; they say, "We don't just want to simply make stuff look good; we want to make smart ideas look great."

Crush Creative's Approach: We have worked with all of the leading publishing houses in London and New York and are lucky in the fact that clients often come to us with a very open brief. We approach cover designs in a few different ways. Sometimes we start with moodboards to set the tone, or create pencil sketches for layout. Other times we go right in for a finished sleeve so that the client can see our idea executed. We don't stick to one style, so the publisher often doesn't know what to expect when they commission us, which makes it fun. We use illustration, photography, collage, type, paint, paper craft, or whatever fits the brief. Once a design is picked, we usually take two or three rounds of corrections before delivering the completed artwork.

Pg 58, all covers: Harper Collins | Pg 59, all covers: Pan Macmillan | Pg 60, all covers: Picador | Pg 61, top left: Chicago Review Press; top right: Chicago Review Press; bottom left: Walker / Canongate; bottom right: Hodder

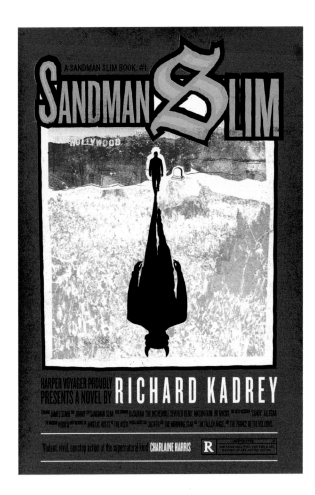

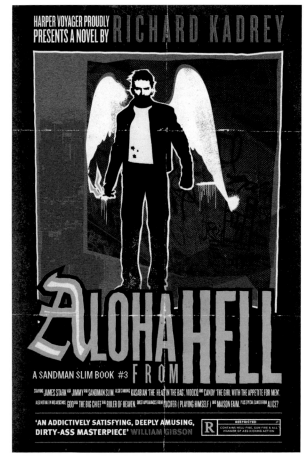

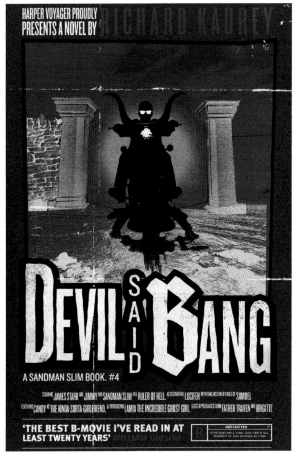

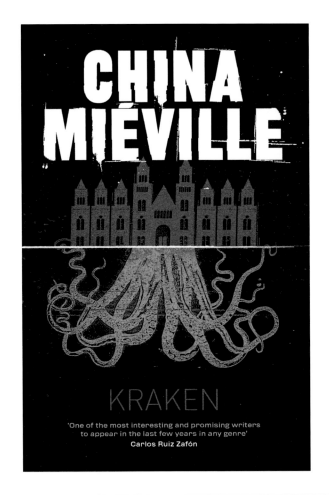

CHINA MIÉVILLE

KRAKEN

'One of the most interesting and promising writers
to appear in the last few years in any genre'
Carlos Ruiz Zafón

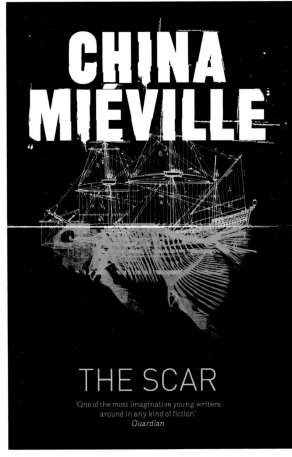

CHINA MIÉVILLE

THE SCAR

'One of the most imaginative young writers
around in any kind of fiction'
Guardian

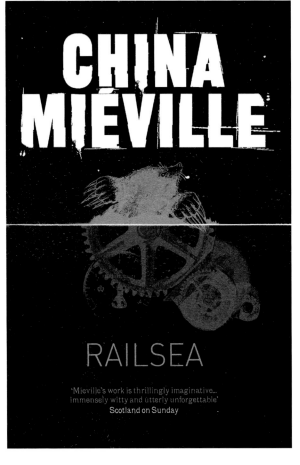

CHINA MIÉVILLE

RAILSEA

'Miéville's work is thrillingly imaginative...
immensely witty and utterly unforgettable'
Scotland on Sunday

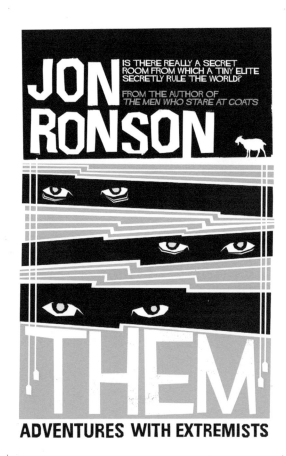

EATING
PEOPLE
IS WRONG

'Brilliantly funny'
Sunday Times

MALCOLM
BRADBURY

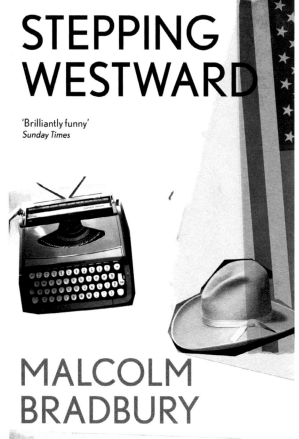

STEPPING
WESTWARD

'Brilliantly funny'
Sunday Times

MALCOLM
BRADBURY

THE
BIBLE

THE BIBLE

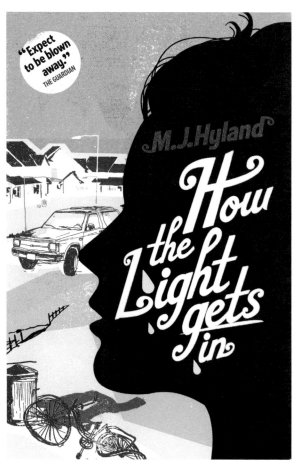

"Expect to be blown away."
THE GUARDIAN

M.J.Hyland

How the Light gets in

David Drummond

David Drummond's company, Salamander Hill Design, was established in 2001 and is located on the second floor of a 200-year-old farm house in rural Quebec. He focuses mainly on book cover design for a wide range of presses. David's clients run the gamut from the small independents up to the bigger publishing houses and university presses. His work has appeared in AIGA, *Communication Arts*, *Print* magazine, and AAUP design competitions.

The Designer's Approach: Because I deal with a wide range of books, it is not always feasible to read the entire book or manuscript. I get access to as much of the manuscript as I need though, and almost always have access to editors and authors, if necessary. Before I put pen to paper I need to find the hook. The hook for me is finding the visual concept that expresses the essence of the book in an unusual way. My goal is to create a "smile in the mind" to quote a well-known book about creative design. I present the book cover design to myself as a visual problem that needs to be solved. At this point, I can turn to other things or projects with the visual problem somewhere in the back of my brain waiting to be solved. This quote from *Mad Men* sums up the creative process perfectly for me: "Just think about it, deeply, and then forget it. An idea will…jump up in your face." –Don Draper to Peggy Olsen

Pg 63, top left: Lincoln Institute of Land Policy; top right: McGill—Queen's University Press; bottom left: McGill—Queen's University Press; bottom right: Vehicule Press | Pg 64, top left: Quai Numero 5; top right: Vehicule Press; bottom left: Vehicule Press; bottom right: McGill—Queen's University Press

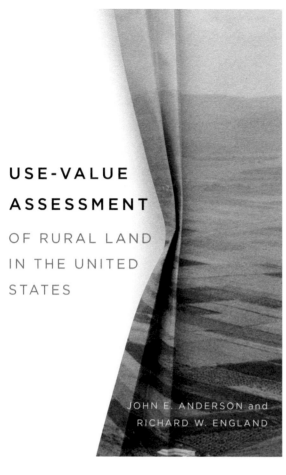

USE-VALUE

ASSESSMENT

OF RURAL LAND
IN THE UNITED
STATES

JOHN E. ANDERSON and
RICHARD W. ENGLAND

JEFFERY DONALDSON

Missing Link

*The Evolution of Metaphor and
the Metaphor of Evolution*

Wet Apples, White Blood   Naomi Guttman

Jim Johnstone

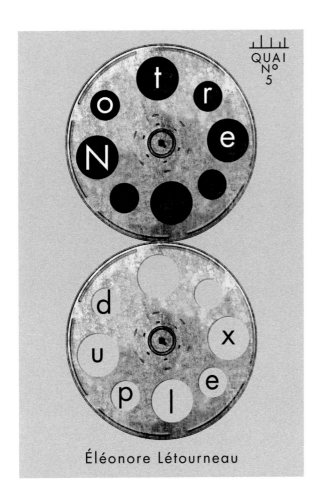

Éléonore Létourneau

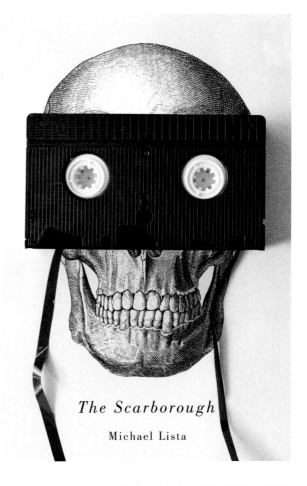

The Scarborough

Michael Lista

a novel

Nicholas Maes

Dead Man's Float

Is this how it ends?

I'm in my bedroom, or was a moment ago. My dressing gown is around my ankles and my underwear is halfway on. The ████████████████████████ stove, as is the bureau with the Meissen figures. The window is shimmering: the elm outside and the street with its houses appear to be resting at the bottom of a river. And, *Gottverdomme!* My legs, my arms, my head, my... my boundaries! They're water, water, everything is water! I can't... I have no... everywhere, yes everywhere...!

My mother, dressed in yellow, swings me in circles.... My father, Dad, he's reading in his armchair.... My uncle's request that I hear his last confession, the pang of thirst when I found out they'd been killed, my meeting with Pete inside the Hotel Manhattan, the derelict my wife almost crushed with our Buick, Netti's cry of exultation, his suicide by gas dear God, and floating at the center, gloating at the center, his face, his, when he met his rock 'n' roll maker....

Memories. I'm floating in my memories, each so fresh

Michael Penny

David A. Gee

David A. Gee has been designing books part-time at night—sometimes late at night—since 2007. He no longer works in advertising, but he still lives in Toronto.

The Designer's Approach: I wish I had a design process. I don't have rituals, or follow a predetermined chain of events in order to arrive at a solution to a brief. Here's how it usually happens: publisher asks if I would like to design a cover for a book. I say, "Yes!" and somehow find the time to do it. It's the same as working in advertising, which I used to do, in that you will always find the answer buried in the brief, no matter how overwritten or under-considered said brief may be. The truth is always somewhere in the middle, and all you have to do is learn how to know when you've seen it.

Think about the problem when you can, scribble down ideas when you can, and if none of that works, just try to make your work look good. Bare-bones competence goes a long way.

Pg 66, top left: ECW Press; top right: ECW Press; bottom left: Harper Collins Canada, Art director: Alan Jones; bottom right: Pluto Books, Art director: Melanie Patrick | Pg 67, all covers: ECW Press / Joyland | Pg 68: Verso Books, Art director: Andy Pressman

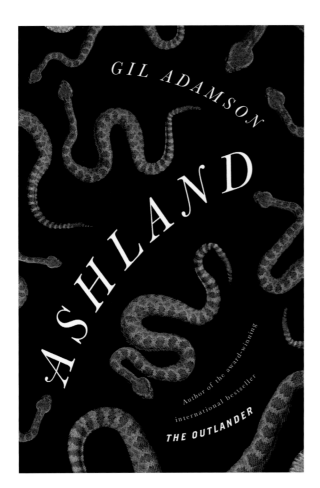

GIL ADAMSON

ASHLAND

Author of the award-winning
international bestseller
THE OUTLANDER

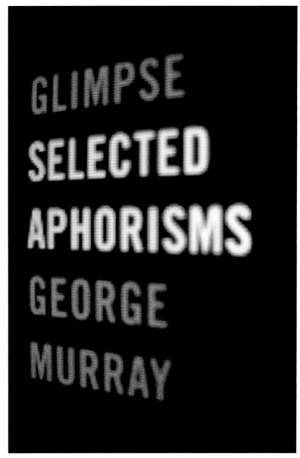

GLIMPSE
SELECTED
APHORISMS
GEORGE
MURRAY

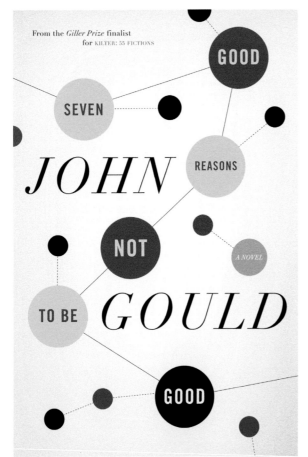

From the *Giller Prize* finalist
for KILTER: 55 FICTIONS

GOOD

SEVEN

JOHN

REASONS

NOT

A NOVEL

TO BE

GOULD

GOOD

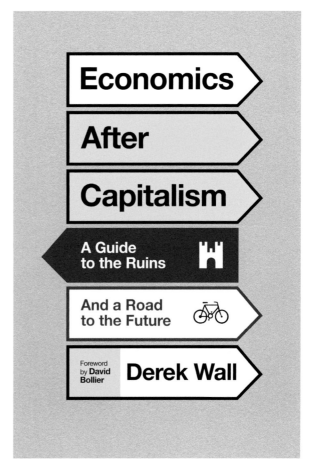

Economics

After

Capitalism

A Guide
to the Ruins

And a Road
to the Future

Foreword
by **David**
Bollier

Derek Wall

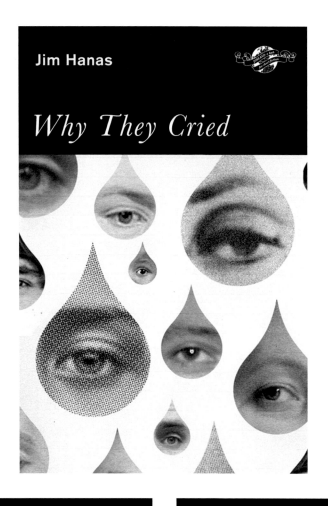

Jim Hanas

Why They Cried

Natalee Caple

How I Came to Haunt My Parents

Megan Stielstra

Everyone Remain Calm

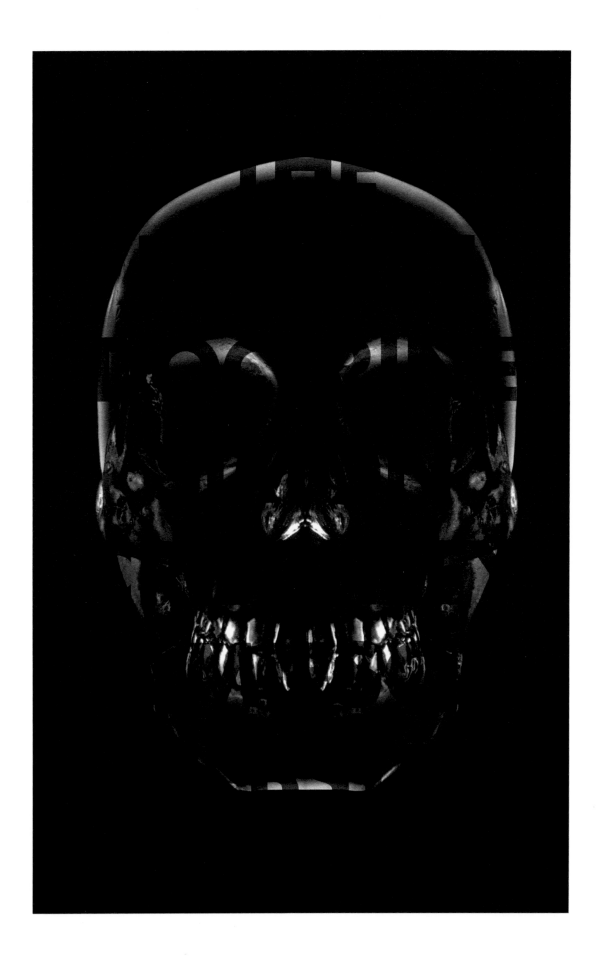

David High

After leaving his native Miami for the bright lights of New York City some twenty-five-odd years ago, David High's passion for books led him straight to the doors of the publishing industry. His award-winning designs have been commissioned by most of the major publishing houses, and he has, through the years, also acted as an out-of-house art director for Basic Books, Bloomsbury, Ecco, and W. W. Norton. David has co-authored two books with his photographer-partner, Ralph Del Pozzo, for Harper Collins Design. Now living upstate, he is close enough to the commuter train to be able to come to terms with the fact that he is now living upstate. He has grown a full beard.

The Designer's Approach: My process is pretty much the same for every book: Read as much of the manuscript as is available and initially do what I think is best for the book, using the ideas that come while reading. Go over notes from client/editor/author and second-guess everything. Do a "gagillion" alternates. Rest. Look at everything fresh and try to edit down. Procrastinate. Panic. Do some frantic-last-minute-down-to-the-wire solutions. (Ironically, it is usually my very first or very last designs that are favored.) SAVE everything. Many killed designs have been resurrected from the flames of utter rejection, and clients are notorious for going full-round-rosy in this industry.

Pg 70, top left: W. W. Norton; top right: Simon and Schuster Photography: Ralph C. Del Pozzo; bottom left: W. W. Norton; bottom right: W. W. Norton I Pg 71: W. W. Norton I Pg 72, all covers: W. W. Norton

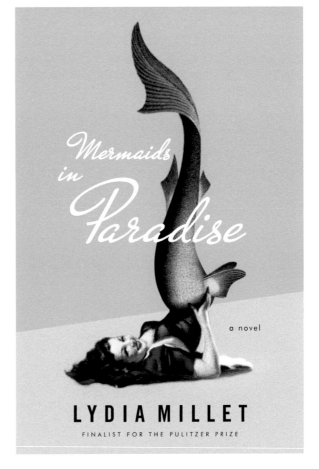

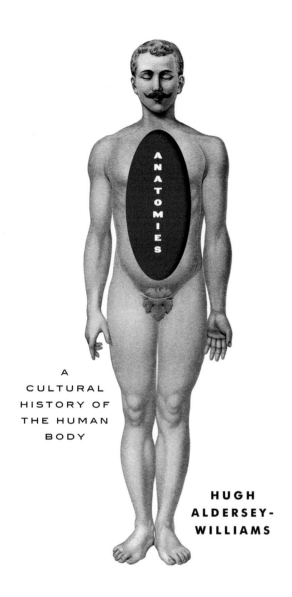

A
CULTURAL
HISTORY OF
THE HUMAN
BODY

HUGH
ALDERSEY-
WILLIAMS

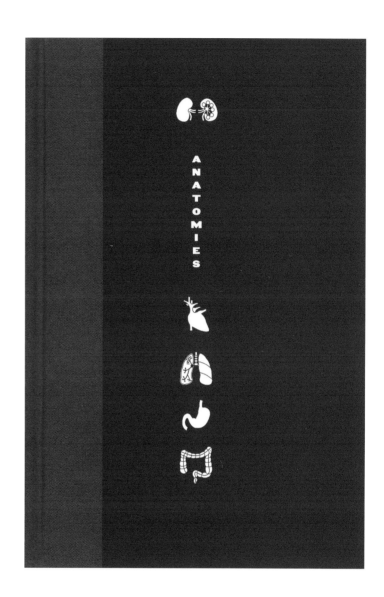

Bernard Cooper

My Avant-Garde Education

a memoir

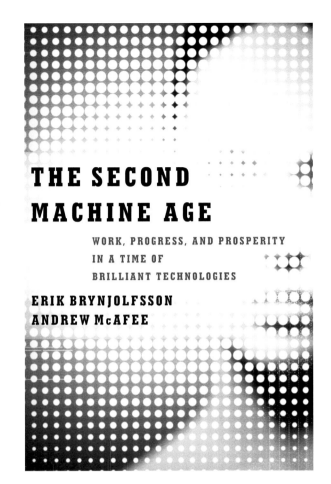

THE SECOND MACHINE AGE

WORK, PROGRESS, AND PROSPERITY
IN A TIME OF
BRILLIANT TECHNOLOGIES

ERIK BRYNJOLFSSON
ANDREW McAFEE

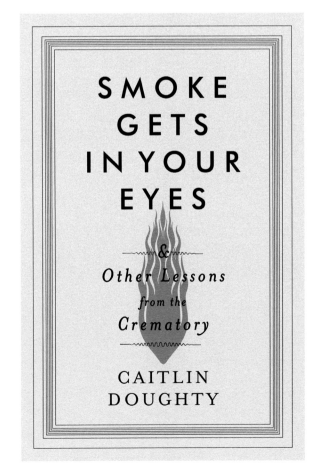

SMOKE
GETS
IN YOUR
EYES

&

Other Lessons
from the
Crematory

CAITLIN
DOUGHTY

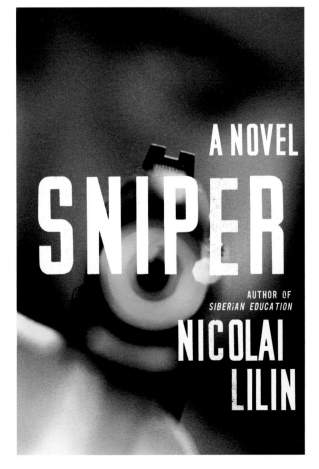

A NOVEL

SNIPER

AUTHOR OF
SIBERIAN EDUCATION

NICOLAI
LILIN

Emily Mahon

A Philadelphia native, **Emily Mahon** studied graphic design and Spanish at Penn State before relocating to New York City. She began her career in publishing and became an art director at Doubleday Books in 2006. Emily's work has been honored with awards from AIGA, The Type Director's Club, The Art Director's Club, and the New York Book Show. She has been published in *Communication Arts* and *Graphis* and *Print*, among others. Emily resides in Brooklyn, New York, with her husband and son.

The Designer's Approach: In designing a book cover, I first read the book. While this may seem an obvious process, I try in my reading to hone in on the book's key elements. I need to gain a sense of the tone and style of writing, the audience the author is trying to reach, and the elements in the story that lend themselves to an inspired design that captures the book's essence. I then spend considerable time thinking about how to best present the book's essence through an image. Since there are so many ways to interpret a book visually, this becomes a wide-open process. I usually start by deciding whether the book should be illustrated or should use photography, or whether to create type or images by hand or digitally. A strong initial concept needs to guide this process.

    The goal in designing any book is creating something that someone will want to pick up and read and, perhaps, return to the cover over and over. Book design means communicating clearly through a visually captivating image, one that captures a book's essence and helps the book leap off the shelves into a reader's hands.

Pg 74, top left: Doubleday, Illustration: Rizon Parein; top right: Anchor; bottom left: Anchor, Photograph: Lesley Unruh; bottom right: Anchor, Photograph of paper snowflake: Laura Hanifin | Pg 75, left: Doubleday; right: Penguin | Pg 76, top left: Anchor; top right: Doubleday, Photograph: Andrew Purcell; bottom left: Spiegel & Grau, Photograph: Chris Stein; bottom right: Penguin, Cover painting: Mari Katogi

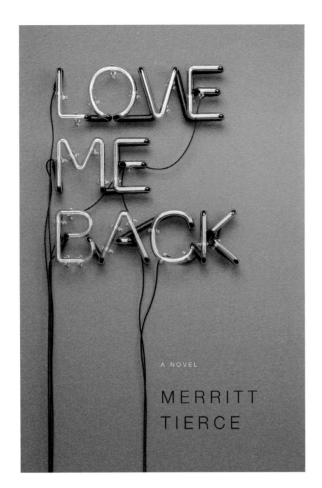

THE WORD EXCHANGE

A NØVEL

ALENA GRAEDON

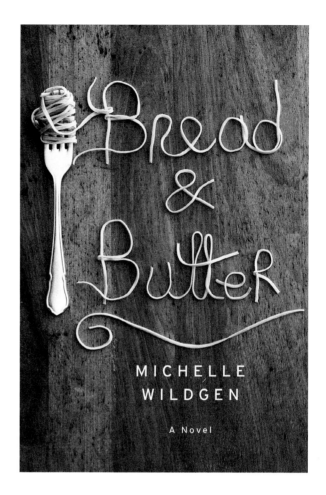

Bread & Butter

MICHELLE WILDGEN

A Novel

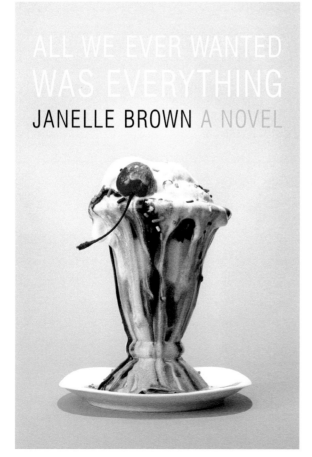

ALL WE EVER WANTED
WAS EVERYTHING
JANELLE BROWN   A NOVEL

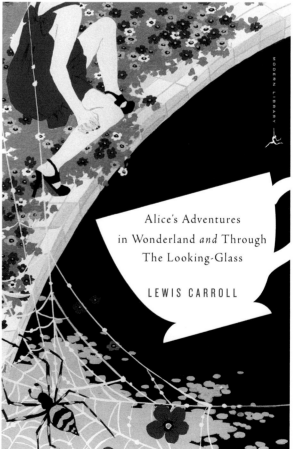

Alice's Adventures
in Wonderland *and* Through
The Looking-Glass

LEWIS CARROLL

Ferran López

Ferran López was born in Barcelona in 1966. He studied photography and combined that profession with graphic design until the year 2001. From that year on, Ferran has been fully dedicated to editorial design. He worked for more than ten years in the Art Department at Random House Spain as a senior designer. At present, since 2012, he is the creative director at Grupo Editorial Planeta.

The Designer's Approach: I am not aware of having a definite creative method, but I must have one. Basically, I try to discover the message the books intend to give, the idea behind the story—this usually happens after "interrogating" the briefing. I underline, take notes, cut...until I grasp the information. At the same time, I imagine who the reader will be and I determine which technique I will apply in the cover design.

Nevertheless, if an idea or a concept does not pop into my head, in spite of draining out all my resources, I just start working the title with typeface, then the author, and voilà, all of a sudden the riddle gets solved and the image appears...almost every time.

Pg 78, **top left:** Planeta / Grupo Planeta, Illustration: Tjalf Sparnaay; **top right:** Destino / Grupo Planeta, Illustration: A&M; **bottom:** Península / Grupo Planeta, Illustration: Adrià Fruitós | **Pg 79, left:** Plaza & Janés / Random House Mondadori, Illustration: Santiago Caruso; **right:** Plaza & Janés / Random House Mondadori, Illustration: Olaf Hajek | **Pg 80, top left:** Grijalbo/Random House Mondadori; **top right:** Plaza & Janés/Random House Mondadori, Photography: Mike Dobela/Arcangel Images; **bottom left:** Grijalbo / Random House Mondadori, Photography: Andrea Hübner; **bottom right:** Caballo de Troya/Random House Mondadori

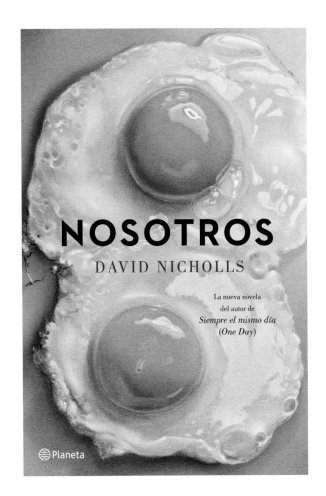

NOSOTROS

DAVID NICHOLLS

La nueva novela
del autor de
Siempre el mismo día
(One Day)

Planeta

Los corruptores
Jorge Zepeda
Patterson

DESTINO

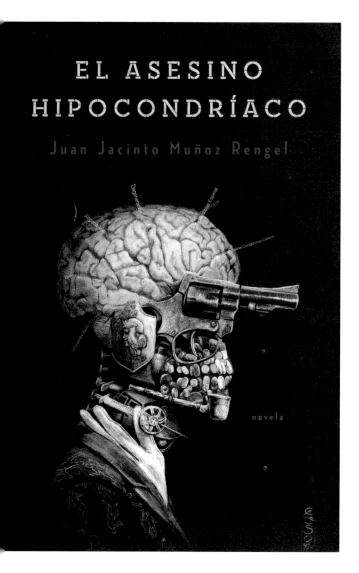

EL ASESINO
HIPOCONDRÍACO

Juan Jacinto Muñoz Rengel

novela

CRISTINA
LÓPEZ BARRIO

LA CASA DE LOS
AMORES
IMPOSIBLES

NOVELA

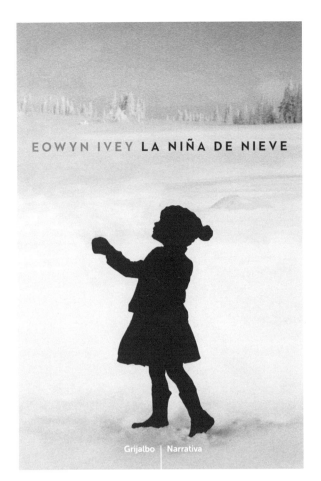

EOWYN IVEY **LA NIÑA DE NIEVE**

Grijalbo | Narrativa

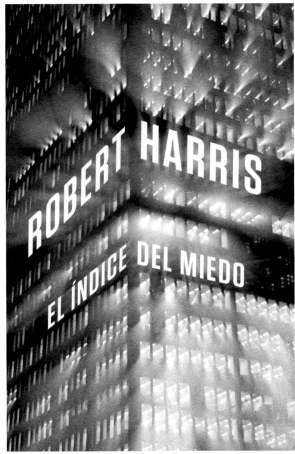

ROBERT HARRIS

EL ÍNDICE DEL MIEDO

LINDA, COMO EN EL ASESINATO DE LINDA

LEIF GW PERSSON

DESPACIO
REMEDIOS ZAFRA ➚

CABALLO DE TROYA

FORT

Established in 1997, **FORT** (formerly Base Art Co.) is a creative agency specializing in print, branding, and digital. The firm's work has been recognized by AIGA, *Communications Arts*, *HOW* magazine, *Print*, numerous books on design, and more. FORT has been designing covers for most of the major trade publishers from the beginning.

FORT's Approach: Terry Rohrbach, owner of **FORT**, recalls: In an attempt to break into the cover design niche, an art director stressed that cover design is pure marketing—that the cover is the promotional billboard as a book sits on a shelf amongst its competitors. That has influenced our work eighteen years later with the goal of capturing the essence of the book in a manner that captivates, is visually appealing, and entices the consumer to pick up the book and dive deeper. The creative process is, I'm sure, like most cover designers—scour the manuscript in search of relevance, sketch ideas, and execute the concept to best represent the book.

Pg 82, top left: The Library of America, Designer: Meredith Reuter; top right: Vintage, Designers: Meredith Reuter, Terry Rohrbach, Drue Dixon; bottom left: Encounter Books, Designer: Meredith Reuter; bottom right: TOR, Designer: Drue Dixon | Pg 83, top left: Hachette Book Group, Designer: Drue Dixon; top right: Penguin Group (USA) LLC, Designer: Terry Rohrbach; bottom left: Random House LLC, Designer: Drue Dixon; bottom right: HarperCollins Publishers, Designers: Terry Rohrbach | Pg 84, top: TOR, Designer: Terry Rohrbach; bottom left: Penguin Group (USA) LLC, Designer: Drue Dixon; bottom right: Self-published, Designer: Terry Rohrbach, Drue Dixon

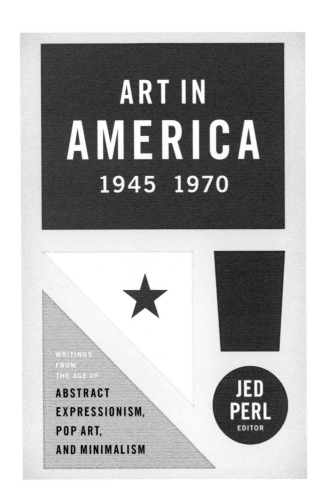

ART IN
AMERICA
1945 1970

WRITINGS
FROM
THE AGE OF
ABSTRACT
EXPRESSIONISM,
POP ART,
AND MINIMALISM

JED
PERL
EDITOR

"Ambitious...convincing...an encyclopedic survey
of the life of the mind in the United States."
— THE NEW YORK TIMES BOOK REVIEW

AMERICA
THE PHILOSOPHICAL

CARLIN ROMANO

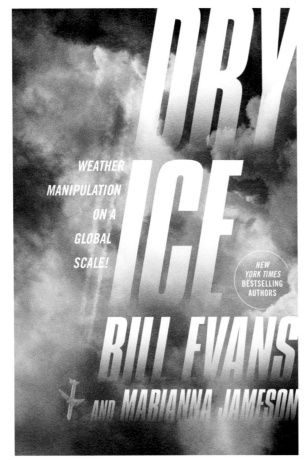

DRY
ICE

WEATHER
MANIPULATION
ON A
GLOBAL
SCALE!

NEW
YORK TIMES
BESTSELLING
AUTHORS

BILL EVANS
AND MARIANNA JAMESON

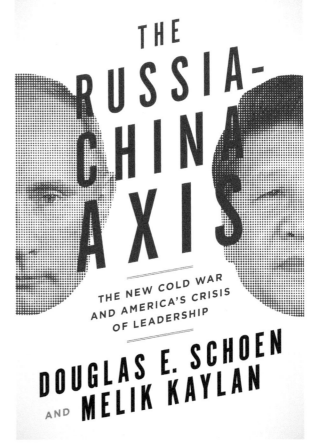

THE
RUSSIA-
CHINA
AXIS

THE NEW COLD WAR
AND AMERICA'S CRISIS
OF LEADERSHIP

DOUGLAS E. SCHOEN
AND MELIK KAYLAN

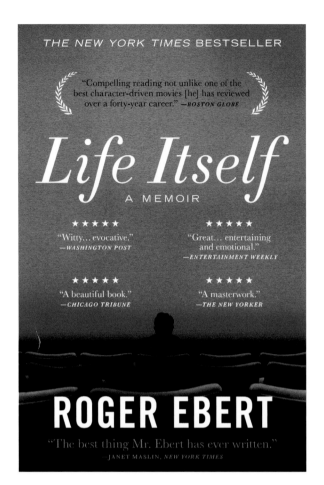

THE NEW YORK TIMES BESTSELLER

"Compelling reading not unlike one of the
best character-driven movies [he] has reviewed
over a forty-year career." —BOSTON GLOBE

Life Itself
A MEMOIR

★★★★★
"Witty... evocative."
—WASHINGTON POST

★★★★★
"Great... entertaining
and emotional."
—ENTERTAINMENT WEEKLY

★★★★★
"A beautiful book."
—CHICAGO TRIBUNE

★★★★★
"A masterwork."
—THE NEW YORKER

ROGER EBERT

"The best thing Mr. Ebert has ever written."
—JANET MASLIN, NEW YORK TIMES

BESTSELLING AUTHOR OF
THE SECRET LIFE OF BEES

Sue Monk Kidd

A Novel

The Invention of Wings

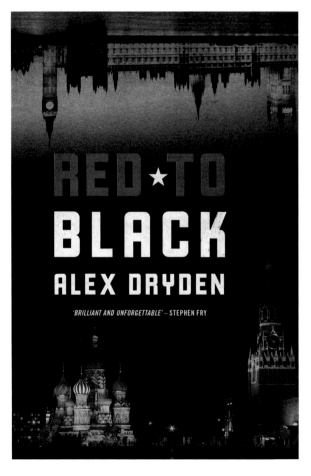

RED ★ TO BLACK

ALEX DRYDEN

'BRILLIANT AND UNFORGETTABLE' – STEPHEN FRY

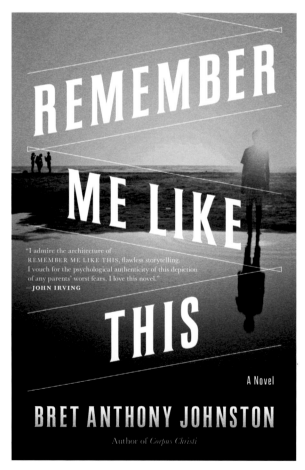

REMEMBER ME LIKE THIS

"I admire the architecture of
REMEMBER ME LIKE THIS, flawless storytelling.
I vouch for the psychological authenticity of this depiction
of any parents' worst fears. I love this novel."
—JOHN IRVING

A Novel

BRET ANTHONY JOHNSTON
Author of Corpus Christi

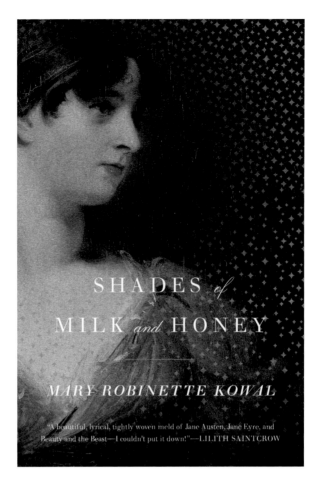

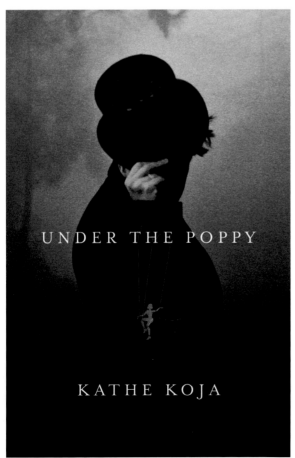

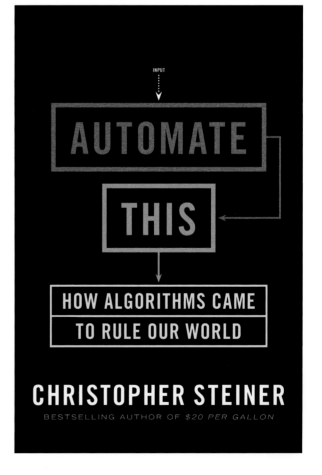

Helen Yentus

Helen Yentus is the art director of Riverhead Books and has been designing book covers for over a decade. Her work has been featured in *Print* magazine, *Graphis*, *Communication Arts*, and *Creative Review*, and by the London Design Museum and the AIGA. In 2007, she was named as one of *Print's* "20 under 30." Most recently, she received an Art Director's Club silver award of Art + Craft in advertising and design.

The Designer's Approach: I begin every single project with the absolute certainty that I have no idea how to design. From there I generally panic and spend weeks procrastinating. Once the realization that I'm completely out of time dawns on me, I begin to work frantically, while kicking myself for not having started earlier, because now I don't have enough time to make what I want to make, the way I want to make it. Over the years, I've come to embrace this as my "process." Sometimes all the panic produces interesting results. Though it doesn't make for the most calming lifestyle.

Pgs 86-87, all covers: Vintage Books, Art director: John Gall | Pg 88: Riverhead Books, 3D slip case designed with and printed by MakerBot Industries

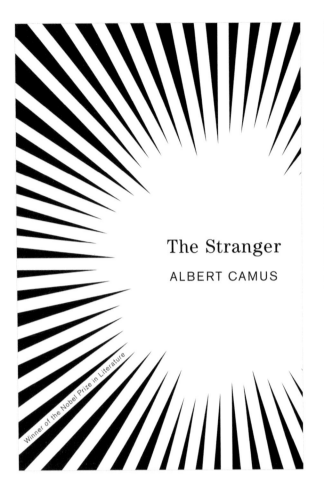

The Stranger

ALBERT CAMUS

Winner of the Nobel Prize in Literature

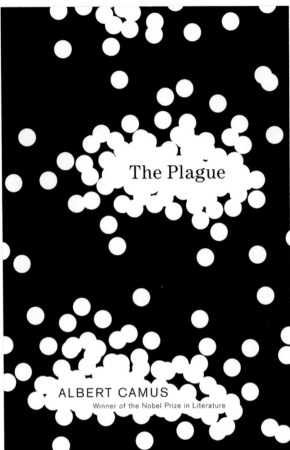

The Plague

ALBERT CAMUS
Winner of the Nobel Prize in Literature

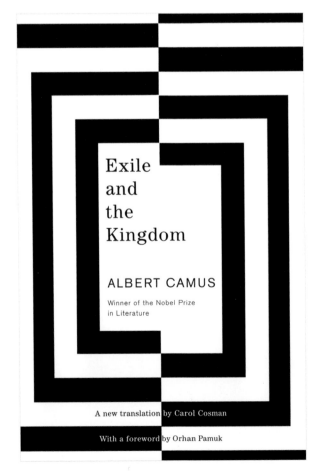

Exile
and
the
Kingdom

ALBERT CAMUS

Winner of the Nobel Prize
in Literature

A new translation by Carol Cosman

With a foreword by Orhan Pamuk

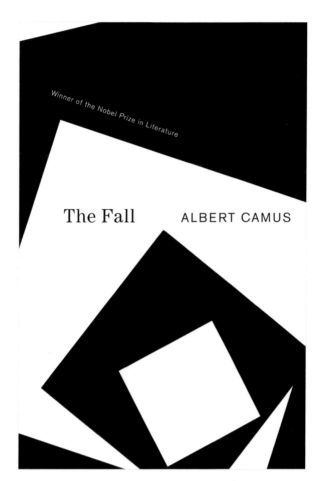

The Fall   ALBERT CAMUS

Winner of the Nobel Prize in Literature

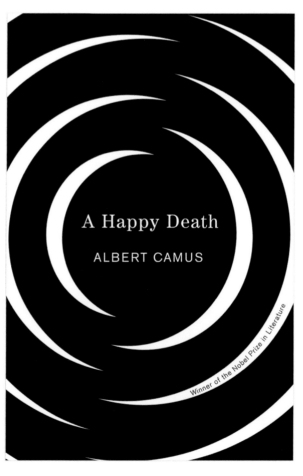

A Happy Death

ALBERT CAMUS

Winner of the Nobel Prize in Literature

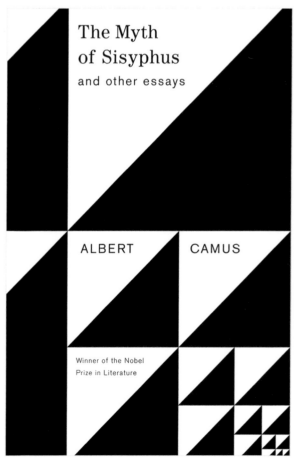

The Myth
of Sisyphus
and other essays

ALBERT   CAMUS

Winner of the Nobel
Prize in Literature

Isaac Tobin

Isaac Tobin is a senior designer at the University of Chicago Press, where he designs books and book covers. He grew up in Hawaii and studied at the Rhode Island School of Design. Isaac's work has been recognized by the AIGA, Type Directors Club, ADC *Young Guns*, STA Archive, and *Print* magazine, among others.

The Designer's Approach: I normally begin my cover designs by reading about the book and crudely sketching the first ideas I get. Sometimes that first idea is cliché and awful, in which case it's useful to get it out of the way; but more often than not, the first idea has a clarity and strength that is very powerful. I try to let the book itself determine my approach to the typography and aesthetics, so that each cover I design is unique.

Pgs 90-92, all covers: The University of Chicago Press, Art director: Jill Shimabukuro

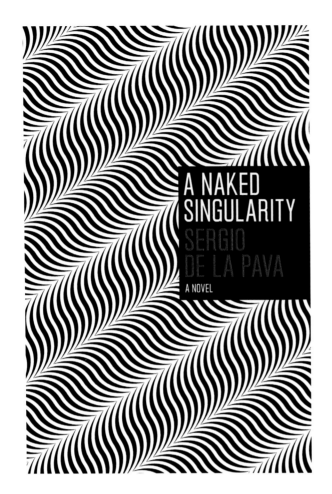

A NAKED
SINGULARITY
SERGIO
DE LA PAVA
A NOVEL

AFTER
FREUD
LEFT

A Century of
Psychoanalysis
in America

EDITED BY
JOHN BURNHAM

An Ethics of Interrogation

MICHAEL SKERKER

THE DAWN
OF THE DEED

*The Prehistoric
Origins of Sex*

JOHN
A. LONG

OBSESSION

A History

LENNARD J.
DAVIS

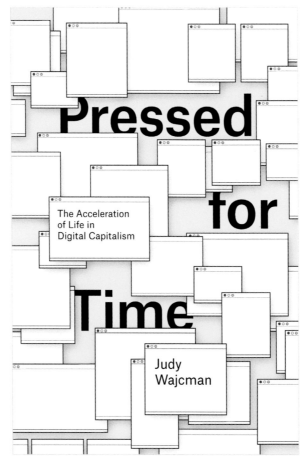

Jacob Covey

For the last decade **Jacob Covey** has been Art Director at Fantagraphics Books, establishing the publisher's reputation for production values and books designed around content. He works from a studio on his farm in Astoria, Oregon.

The Designer's Approach: The most critical thing for me is capturing the tone of a book, which is why typography is so important in my work. The tone encompasses themes but also the voice of the author/ artist. Whether it's a novel or an art monograph, I look for a way to translate the nuance of the work into a more blunt visual shorthand. The goal is to catch the eye of the people who will enjoy this specific book but don't know it yet.

Pg 93: Illustration: Tony Millionaire I **Pg 94, top row:** Fantagraphics, Edited by Gary Groth; **bottom row:** Fantagraphics, Edited by Eric Reynolds I **Pg 95, all covers:** Fantagraphics, Edited by Kim Thompson I **Pg 96, top left:** Fantagraphics, Edited by Gary Groth; **top right:** Abrams, Art director: Michelle Ishay; **bottom left:** Fantagraphics, Edited by Gary Groth; **bottom right:** Ecco, Art director: Allison Saltzman I **Pg 97, top left:** Fantagraphics, Edited by Eric Reynolds; **top right:** Fantagraphics. Edited by Gary Groth. **bottom:** Fantagraphics, Covers by Gilbert and Jaime Hernandez. Edited by Eric Reynolds. The case reproduces the color layer of a comic cover and the acetate overlay outlines the black line art.

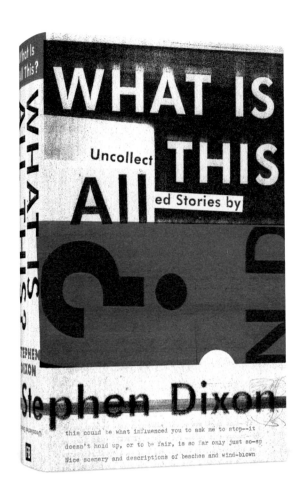

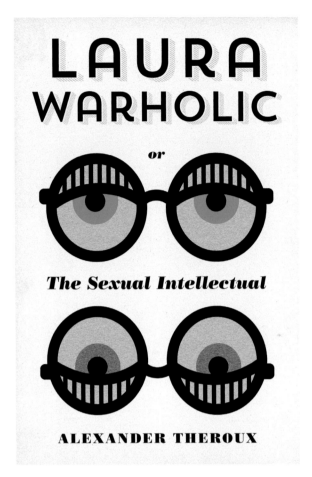

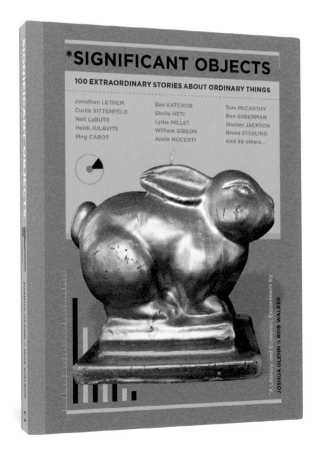

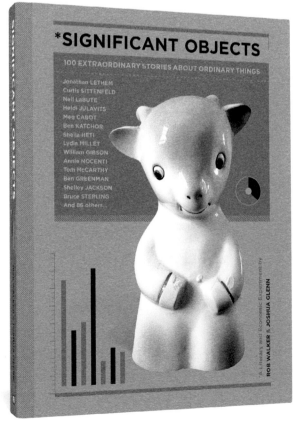

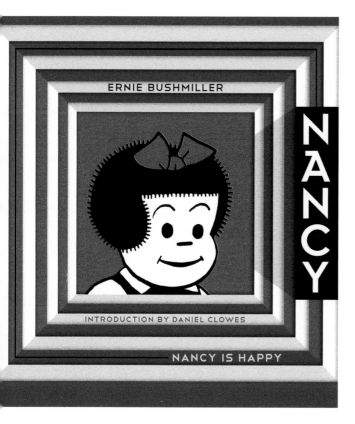

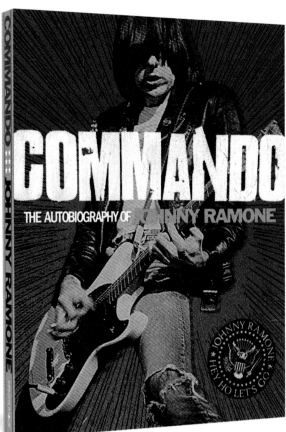

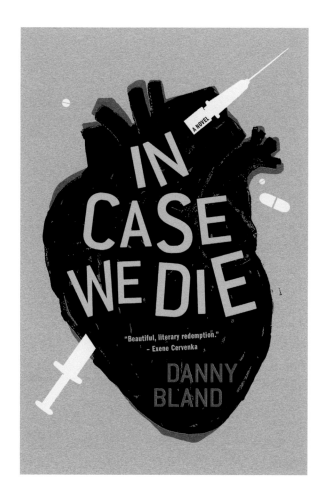

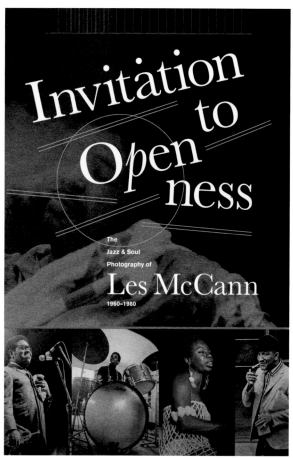

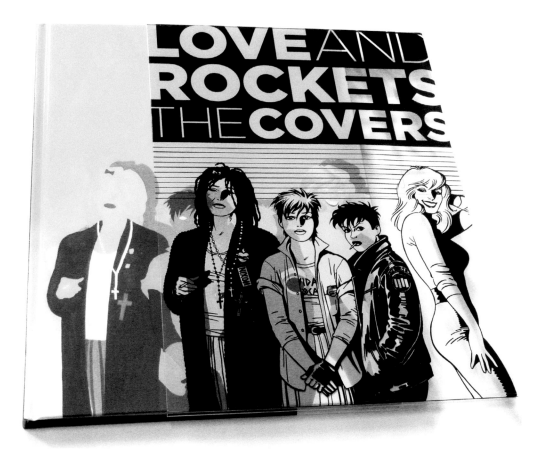

Jamie Keenan

Jamie Keenan is based in London and works mainly for American and British publishers.

The Designer's Approach: The very first thing I do when I work on a book cover (other than reading the book or manuscript) is to write the title and author in pencil and stare at the words for a while. Sometimes this alone conjures up an idea. If that fails—and you have to put some effort into it—it's best to approach the job from a slightly oblique angle. Ideas are like butterflies: if you attempt to hunt them down head on, they fly away and you never see them again, but if you sit there quietly, half-thinking about something else, eventually, one may land on your head.

I'm not very good at making simple things look beautiful, so instead I have to come up with a concept that will form the basis of the whole cover and, from this, choices over things like color schemes and typefaces become automatic—the concept dictates the direction the cover will go in, and because it takes on this life of its own, your role becomes less like an artistic director and more like a zookeeper. The cover mostly looks after itself and you just need to feed it from time to time and clean up when it makes a mess.

Pg 99, left: Harbour Books; right: The Overlook Press | Pg 100, top left: Atticus Books; top right: Vintage; bottom left: Vintage; bottom right: W. W. Norton & Company | Pg 101, top left: Penguin; top right: W. W. Norton & Company; bottom left: Canongate Books Ltd; bottom right: Liveright

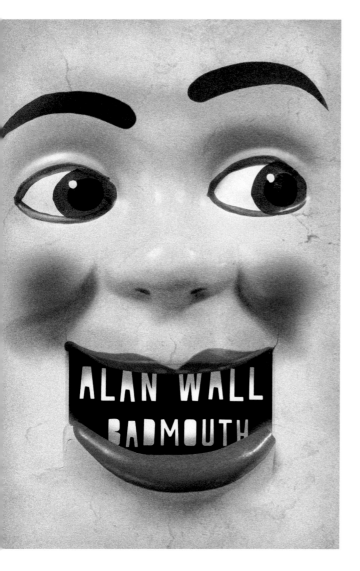

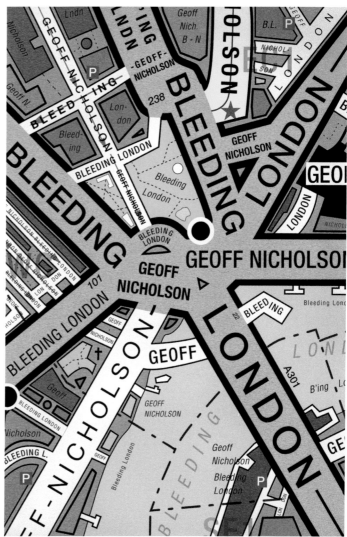

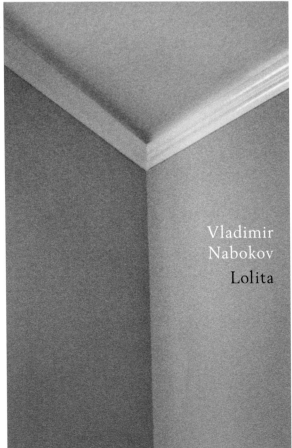

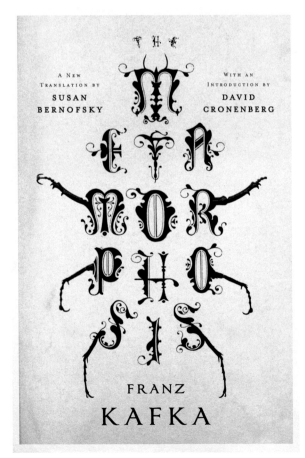

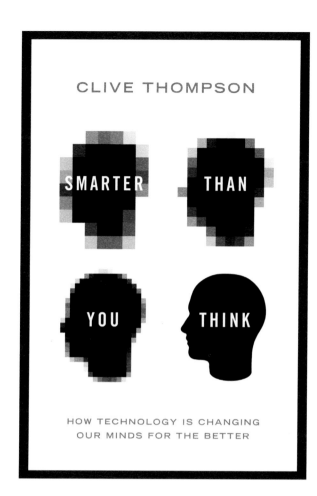

CLIVE THOMPSON

SMARTER THAN

YOU THINK

HOW TECHNOLOGY IS CHANGING
OUR MINDS FOR THE BETTER

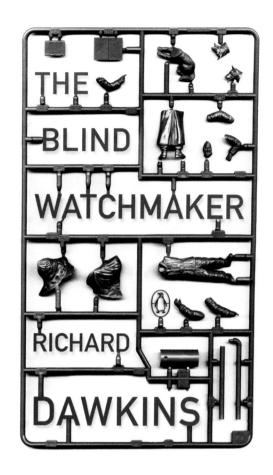

THE
BLIND
WATCHMAKER

RICHARD

DAWKINS

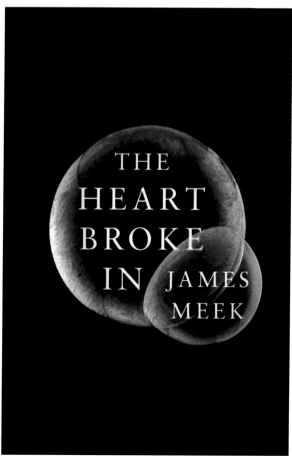

THE
HEART
BROKE
IN JAMES
MEEK

THE WASTE LAND T.S. ELIOT

with an
introduction
by Paul
Muldoon

Jarrod A. Taylor

Jarrod Taylor grew up in the forests of the Pacific Northwest. He went to art school for a couple years in Seattle and learned how to draw. After school, he worked for a few years and then decided to move to New York to attend art school again to learn how to draw *better* pictures. Upon graduating, he somehow found a job drawing pictures on books, and that's what he's been doing ever since.

The Designer's Approach: I don't really have a sole working technique that I rely on, as each new book cover to design brings it's own new challenges with it. When starting a new cover, the main objective seems to be just trying to find what sort of image represents the book in the best way. So my whole process is about finding that image, be it a commissioned illustration, hand-drawn type, or the right stock photo of a woman in peril, etc.

Pg 103: Harper Perennial I Pg 104, **top left:** Harper Perennial; **top right:** W. W. Norton & Company; **bottom left:** Harper Perennial; **bottom right:** Harper Perennial I Pg 105, **top left:** It Books; **top right:** Harper Perennial; **bottom:** Harper Perennial

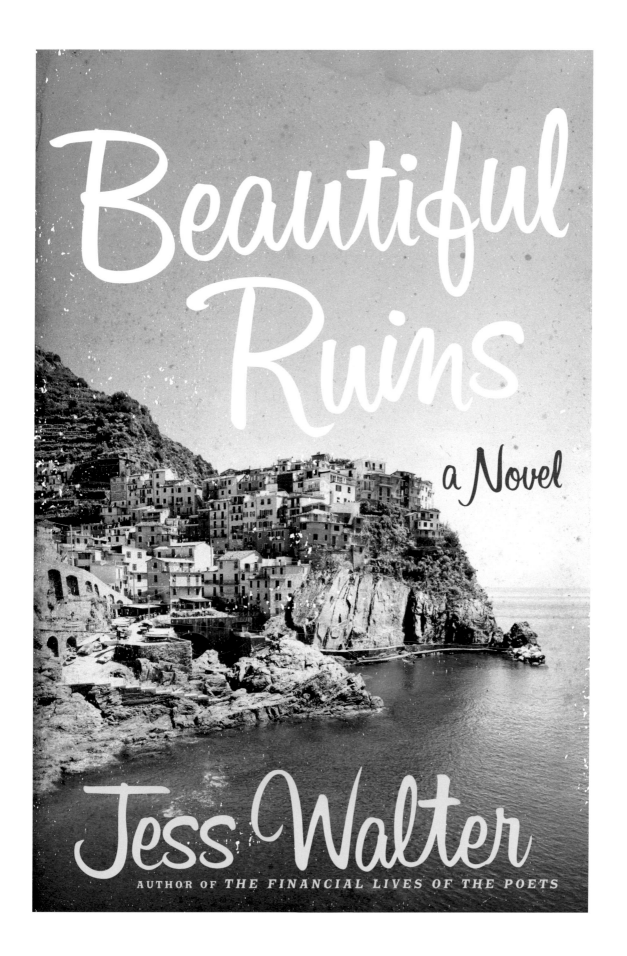

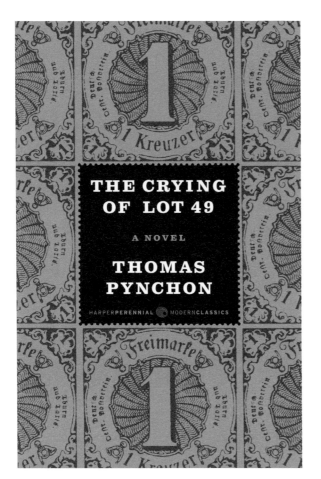

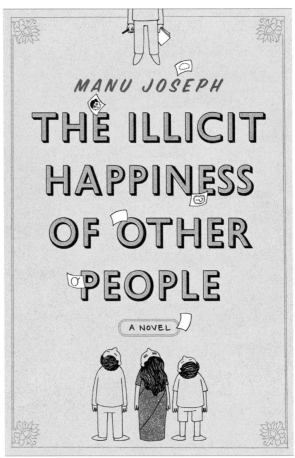

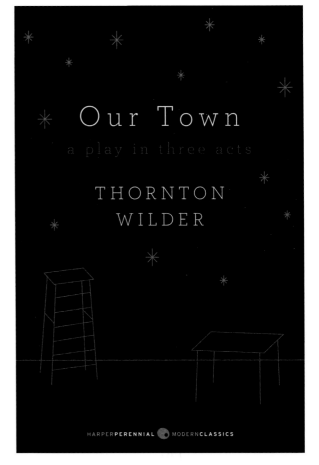

Jason Booher

Jason Booher is the art director of Blue Rider Press. He teaches at Parsons School for Design.

The Designer's Approach: I don't really have a consistent design process. Not for any conceptual reason. It just always seems to be different from book to book. Sometimes I'll start with the type—see what letters and words I have to work with even before I start reading or as I start reading. Often I'll sketch thumbnails before, during, and after the reading.

But I guess most of my solutions come after a close reading of the text and enough time for things to mix about in my head. For lack of a better phrase, I am looking for the soul of the book when I read—what makes it special or different. That's why, if I am stuck, I will go back and reread the manuscript.

And I try as much as possible not to look at contemporary book covers, or even much at contemporary design. I think most successful book covers don't look like other book covers in that moment (or anything from say the last twenty years). It's the single most important thing for a successful package. Even if you are trying to signal a kind of book/genre, you still want the book to feel unique. Having that visually unique package relate to the soul of the book is, of course, the ultimate goal. So I try to derive the visual form in response (and usually it's quite an abstract response) to something in the writing. I don't pretend I'm saying something new here. I would imagine this is what most book cover designers do.

I think the difficulty after a few years of working is trying to find different formal approaches to similar problems. So it is important to take risks, try to have fun; don't solve the problem quickly, or make the cover that you know will satisfy the editor and publisher and author without pushing it and pulling it.

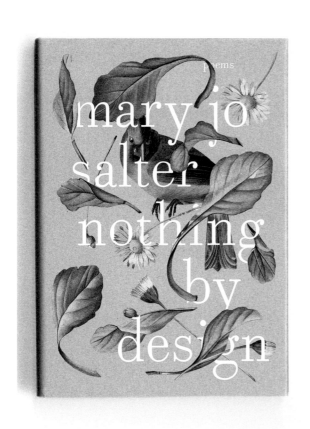

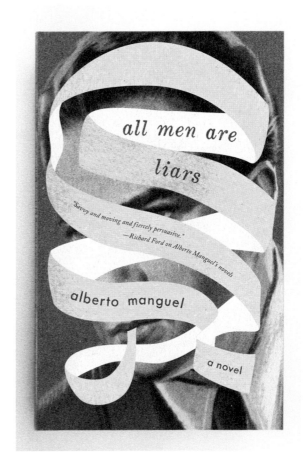

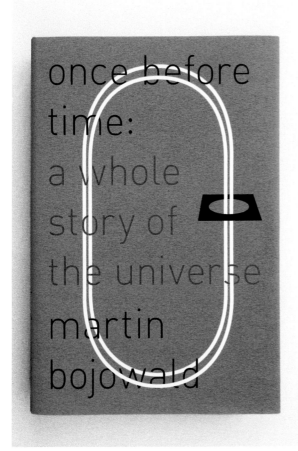

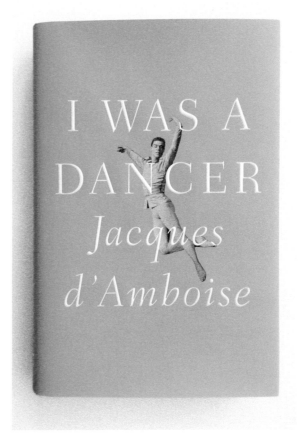

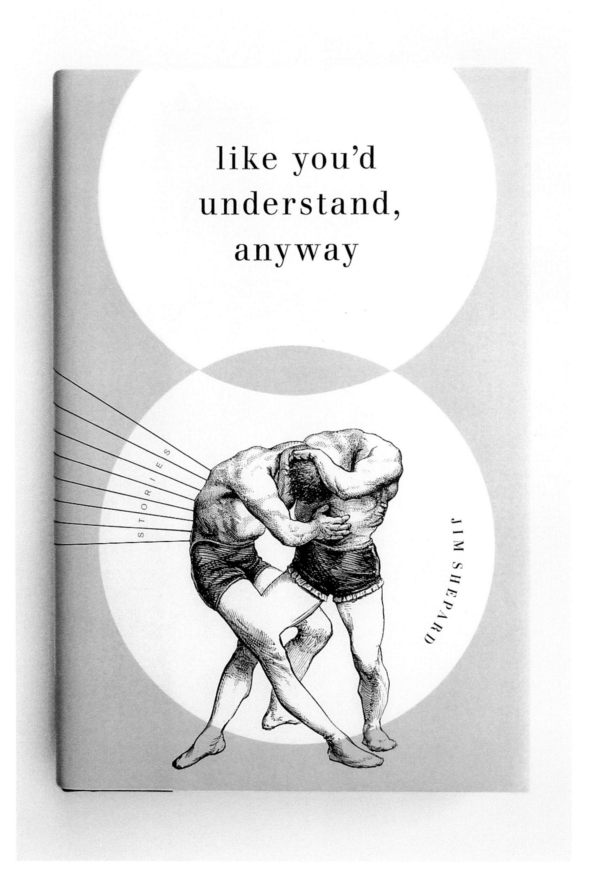

like you'd
understand,
anyway

STORIES

JIM SHEPARD

Frank Rose

The Art
of Immersion

How the digital generation is remaking Hollywood, Madison Avenue, and the way we tell stories

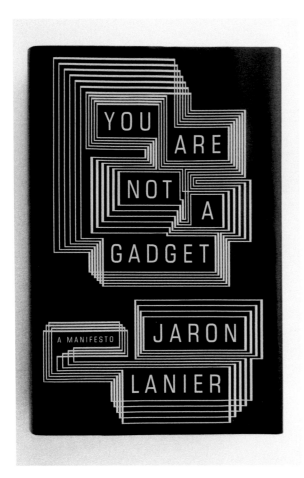

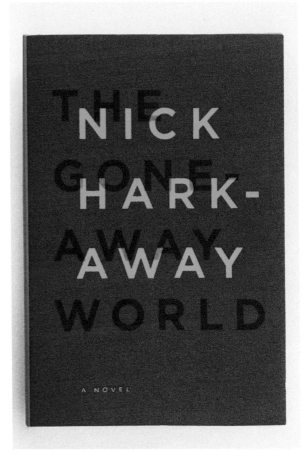

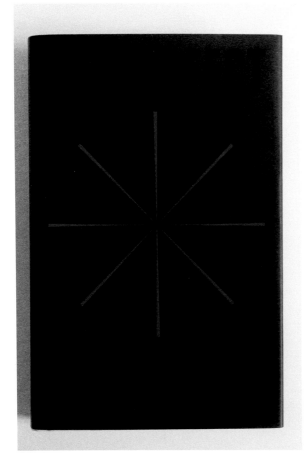

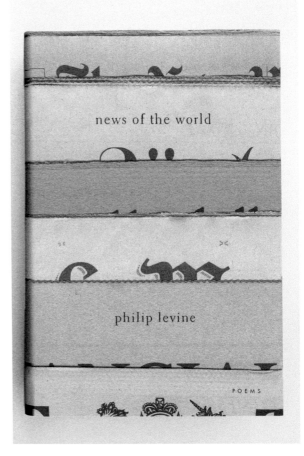

Jason Heuer

Jason Heuer spent over a decade at Simon & Schuster art directing and designing award-winning covers. He now runs his design and art studio, Jason Heuer Design, in Astoria, Queens, with clients such as Random House, MTV, and *The New York Times*. Jason received his BFA for Advertising and Design from the School of Visual Arts where he now teaches typography to undergraduates and tries to get them internships in publishing.

The Designer's Approach: As a designer, I want people to pick up the book because of its cover. I call it "pick-ability or click-ability." If someone picks it up, they are halfway to the register; if someone clicks on the thumbnail, they are halfway to the checkout cart. The challenge is to design within the genre while presenting something new for a customer to discover. People don't give the readers enough credit for their intelligence; they like to have a challenge and engage with a cover—it can be an experience. A reader is looking because they are already interested in books, and I want to give them a reason to choose my cover.

Pgs 112-113: Simon & Schuster, Illustrations: Mark Stutzman I Pg 114: Simon & Schuster, Uncoated paper stock with gold foil I Simon & Schuster, Gold foil detail I Pg 115, top left: Simon & Schuster, Photograph: Isabelle Selby; top right: Simon & Schuster, Simple matte finish; bottom left: Simon & Schuster, Design: Jason Heuer and Andrew D. Kaufman, Photograph: Isabelle Selby; bottom right: Scribner, Day-Glo Pink and Day-Glo Green, matte with spot gloss, Illustration: Jason Heuer I Pg 116: Simon & Schuster, Half-jacket with printed case I Simon & Schuster, Illustrations: Mark Stutzman

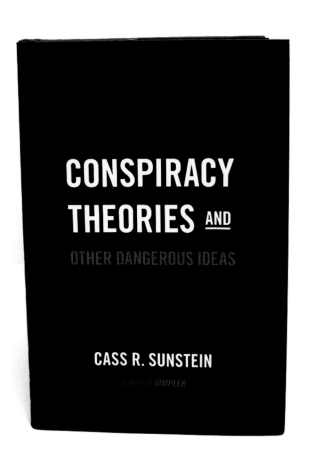

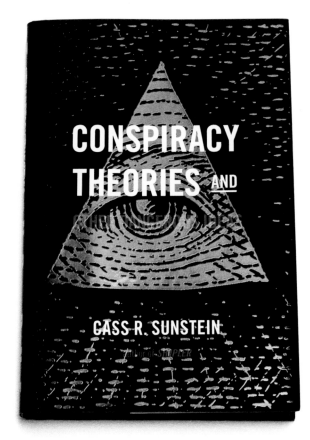

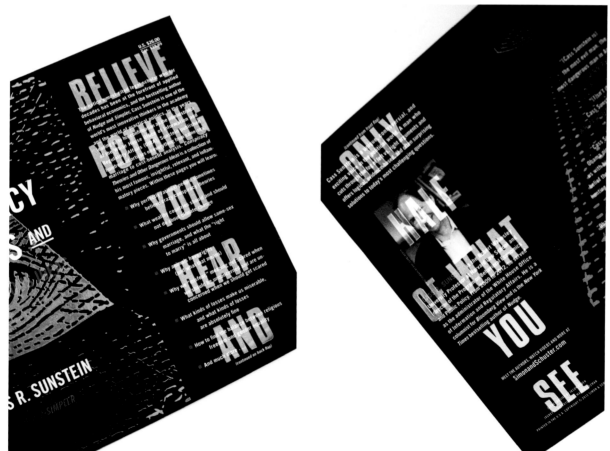

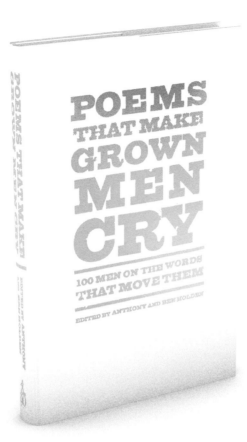

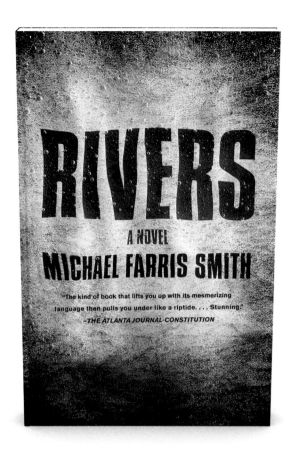

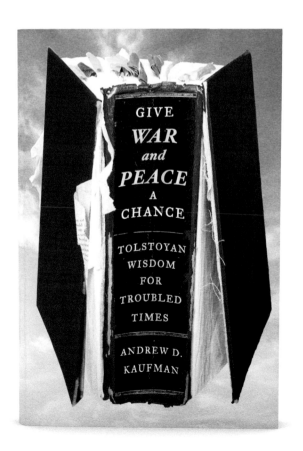

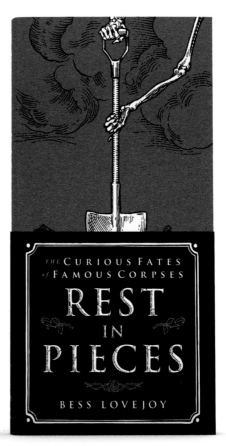

THE CURIOUS FATES
of FAMOUS CORPSES

REST
IN
PIECES

BESS LOVEJOY

Jason Ramirez

Jason Ramirez is a multidisciplinary designer based in New York City. He is currently an art director for Penguin Random House. Previously, he worked with St. Martin's Press and Rodrigo Corral Design in New York. Originally from Kansas, Jason is a graduate of Parsons, The New School for Design, and the University of Rochester. His work has been featured in AIGA's "50 Books/50 Covers," New York Book Show, *Communication Arts*, and *Print* magazine.

The Designer's Approach: For me, the design process includes a few pieces: Read, Research, Brainstorm, Sketch, Execute. Some steps require more time and attention than others. And the process may need to be repeated until the desired outcome. Yet regardless of the recipe, perseverance is often the glue that binds it all together.

Pg 118, top left: Penguin, Art director: Paul Buckley; top right: Penguin, Art director: Paul Buckley; bottom left: Palgrave-Macmillan, Photographer: Jo Whaley, Art director: David Baldeosingh Rotstein; bottom right: The Countryman Press, Art director: Kermit Hummel | Pg 119: Penguin, Art directors: Paul Buckley, Roseanne Serra | Pg 120, top left: Viking, Commemorative edition designed to celebrate the 75th anniversary of the first hardcover publication of Steinbeck's Pulitzer Prize winning epic. The limited edition features specially designed endpapers and a leather case with black foil stamping, as well as a gilded top, and a California Poppy orange ribbon. Illustrator: Michael Schwab, Creative director: Paul Buckley; top right: Penguin, Photography: Gentl and Hyers, Art director: Paul Buckley; bottom left: St. Martin's Press, Art director: David Baldeosingh Rotstein; bottom right: Farrar, Straus and Giroux, Art director: Charlotte Strick

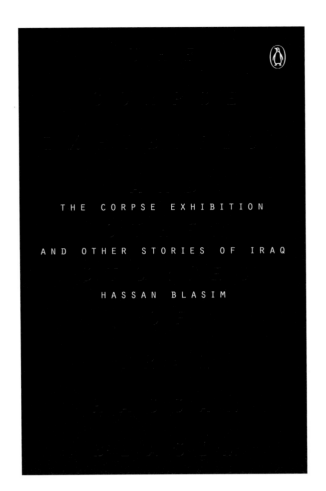

THE CORPSE EXHIBITION

AND OTHER STORIES OF IRAQ

HASSAN BLASIM

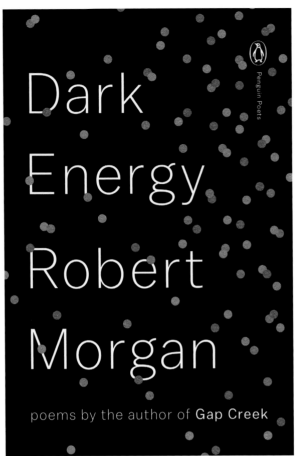

Dark
Energy
Robert
Morgan

poems by the author of **Gap Creek**

Penguin Poets

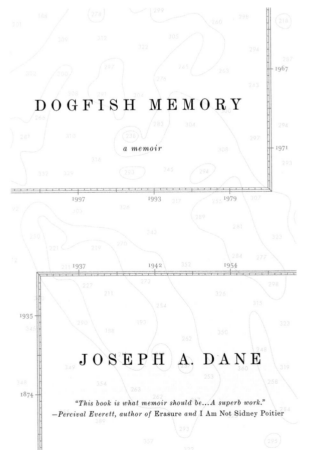

DOGFISH MEMORY

a memoir

JOSEPH A. DANE

"This book is what memoir should be...A superb work."
—*Percival Everett, author of* Erasure *and* I Am Not Sidney Poitier

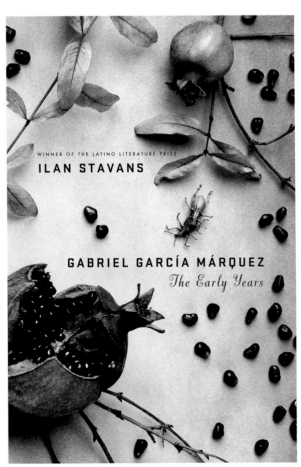

WINNER OF THE LATINO LITERATURE PRIZE

ILAN STAVANS

GABRIEL GARCÍA MÁRQUEZ
The Early Years

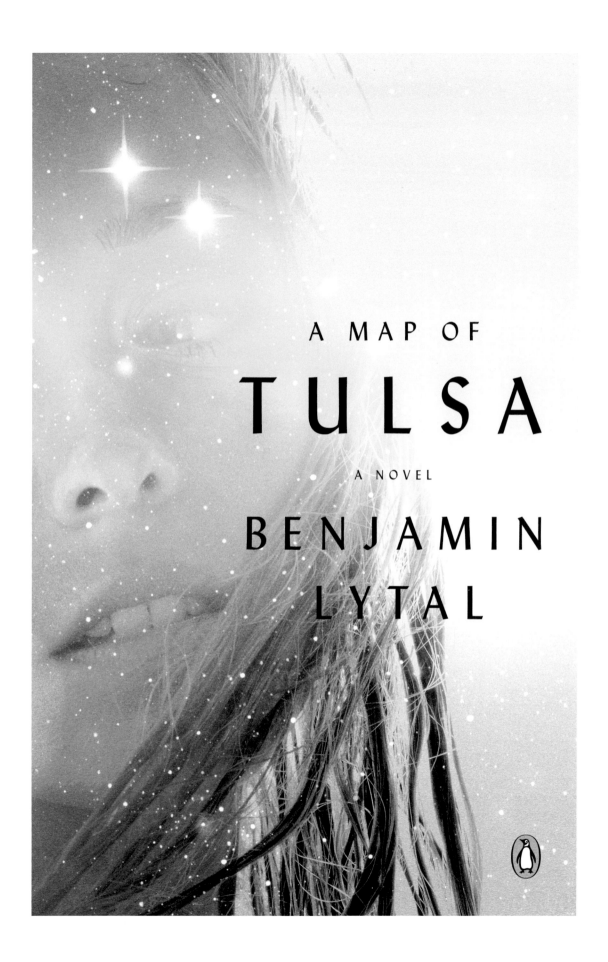

A MAP OF
TULSA

A NOVEL

BENJAMIN
LYTAL

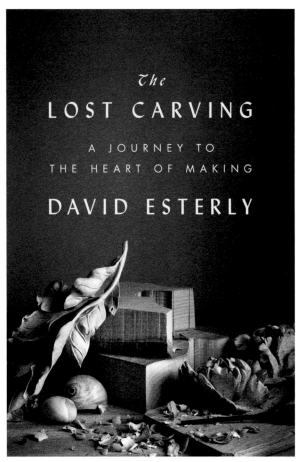

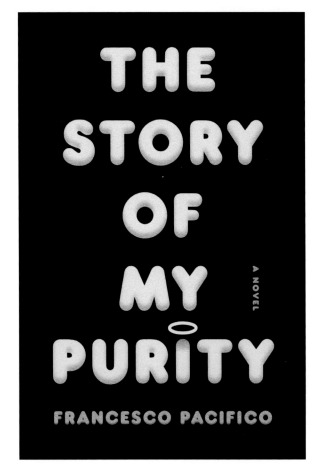

Jennifer Heuer

Jennifer Heuer is a full-time freelance graphic designer working out of the Pencil Factory. She went to Pratt Institute in Brooklyn, worked in-house at HarperCollins, then Simon & Schuster, and now runs her own studio, designing for a variety of publishers as well as teaching at Pratt. She's recently worked with *The New York Times*; Riverhead; Ecco; Little, Brown; W. W. Norton; Scribner; Penguin; Simon & Schuster; Vintage; HarperCollins; Grand Central; Counterpoint Press; Random House; Knopf; and many other publishers.

The Designer's Approach: Every book is different, so the process can vary. But ideally, this is how I hope I'm working: Naturally, I read the manuscript, if there is one. While I'm reading, I keep a running list of keywords, signifiers, and themes in my notebook. I just worked on a nonfiction book about "working life" and started a list of things from uniforms, briefcases, and lunch pails to steam-whistles, coffee breaks, and punch-clocks. I create free-association lists like this, trying to decide on a general direction for the look and concept. Then I head to the library. I'm a Pratt alumni, and their library has a remarkably eclectic collection of odd ball books and a picture library. I'm also a big fan of the New York Public Library's picture collection—so much to pull from. Then I tend to sketch out ideas. I made these simple worksheets: basically six book-shaped rectangles on a sheet of copy paper to knock around some layouts before using the computer. When I'm back in the studio, I set up a moodboard to organize the artwork I've created and keep track of images I've collected. From there it's trying to knock out some layouts based on sketches. That can be setting up a small photo-shoot of objects, or hand-lettering a title, or creating my own illustration. Really, it comes down to a lot of prep work before starting the actual design. That said, sometimes I need to be wary of over-thinking a project and spinning my wheels. Sometimes it's nice to have almost no time at all and just go with my gut. Overall though, this process tends to work from fiction to non-fiction. And, of course, no project is ideally set up to have the kind of time it takes to go through each step—which is why it's good to keep a running catalog of inspiration and ideas.

Pg 122, **top left:** Scribner; **top right:** Riverhead Books, Stitching: Julie Jackson; **bottom left:** Farrar, Straus and Giroux; **bottom right:** W. W. Norton & Company I **Pg 123, all covers:** W. W. Norton & Company I **Pg 124, top left:** W. W. Norton & Company; **top right:** Portfolio; **bottom left:** Columbia University Press; **bottom right:** Liveright

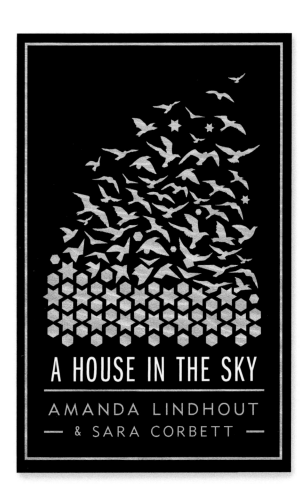

A HOUSE IN THE SKY

AMANDA LINDHOUT
& SARA CORBETT

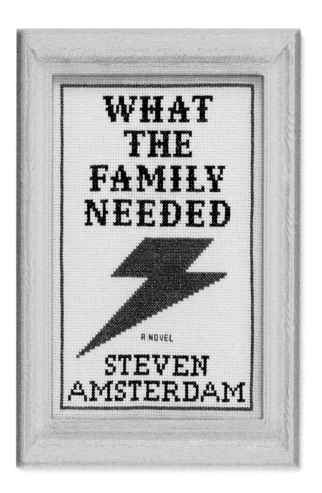

WHAT THE FAMILY NEEDED

A NOVEL

STEVEN AMSTERDAM

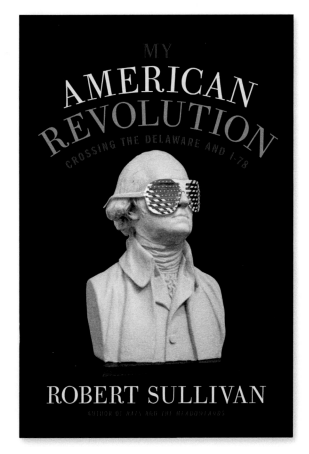

MY AMERICAN REVOLUTION

CROSSING THE DELAWARE AND I-78

ROBERT SULLIVAN

AUTHOR OF RATS AND THE MEADOWLANDS

NIGHT AT THE FIESTAS

STORIES

KIRSTIN VALDEZ QUADE

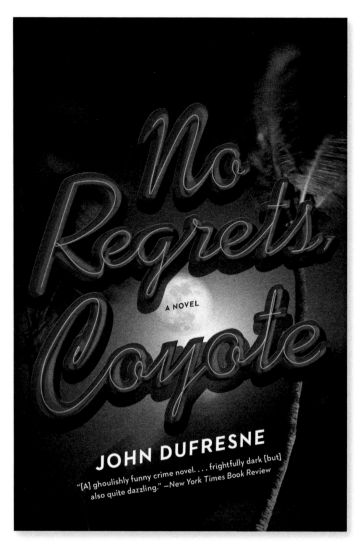

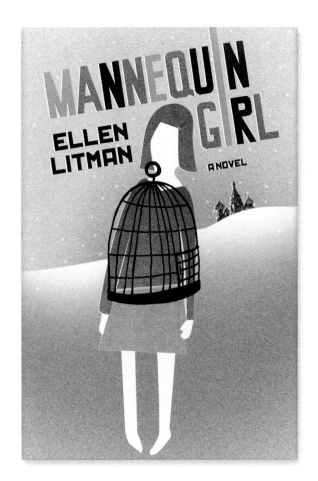

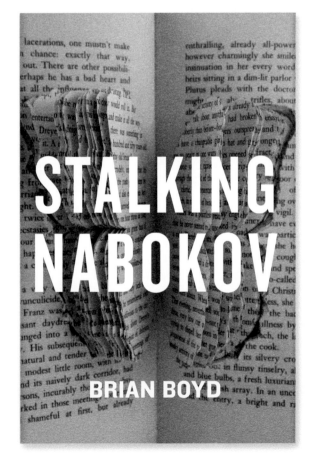

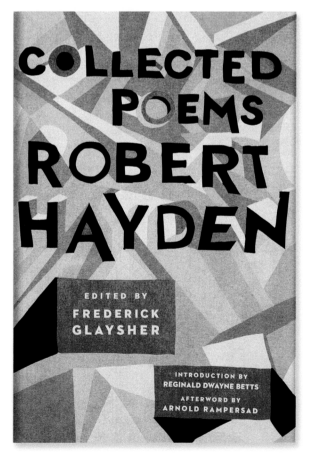

Jenny Carrow

Jennifer Carrow has been designing book covers for over ten years. Originally from Kentucky, she moved to New York to attend the Cooper Union School of Art. She currently designs jackets in-house for Farrar, Straus and Giroux Publishers. Her work has been recognized by the AIGA, ADC, and *Print* magazine.

The Designer's Approach: Some of the jackets I design begin with a very clear idea, some begin with art provided from the author, and others begin as a completely blank page in InDesign. From there, I search all over for art, or create my own, try out the title in many, many different typefaces, print out comps, stare at them on my wall, and continue to add and remove elements until the design feels right for the book. I give myself small challenges with every new list of books, like trying to use neon, make a familiar typeface look new, search for lesser-known photographers, etc. My best advice is to try and sleep on your designs for a night. It really helps to come back to your work with fresh eyes.

Pg 126, top left: Farrar, Straus and Giroux, Art: detail from *Roses* by Sir Roy Calne; top right: Farrar, Straus and Giroux, Jacket photograph: Celeste Jones; bottom left: Farrar, Straus and Giroux; bottom right: Farrar, Straus and Giroux, Jacket painting of red blood cells: Michele Banks | Pg 127: Farrar, Straus and Giroux | Pg 128, top left: Farrar, Straus and Giroux, Jacket art © Fundación Olga y Rufino Tamayo; photograph by Barbara Hoffmeister; top right: Picador; bottom left: Farrar, Straus & Giroux Originals; bottom right: Farrar, Straus and Giroux

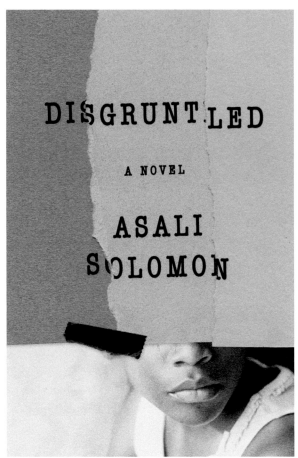

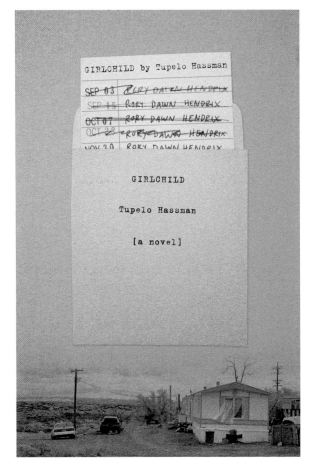

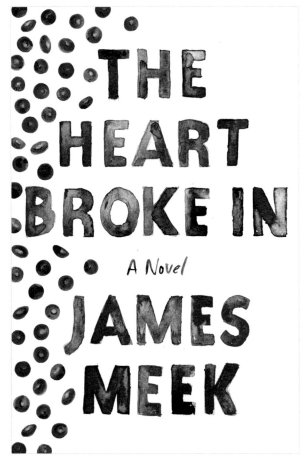

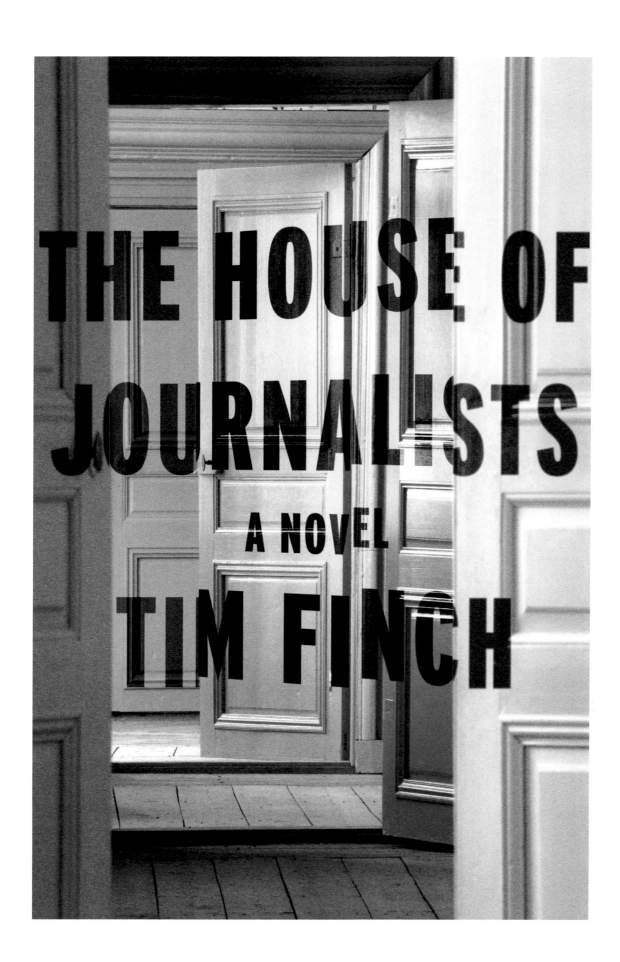

THE HOUSE OF JOURNALISTS

A NOVEL

TIM FINCH

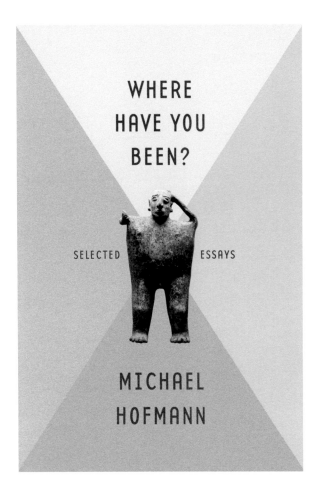

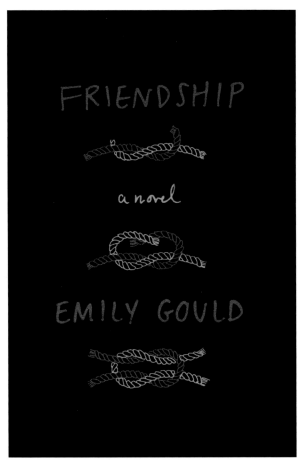

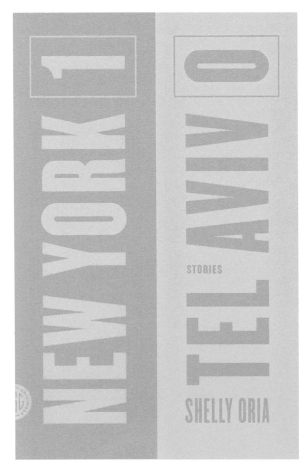

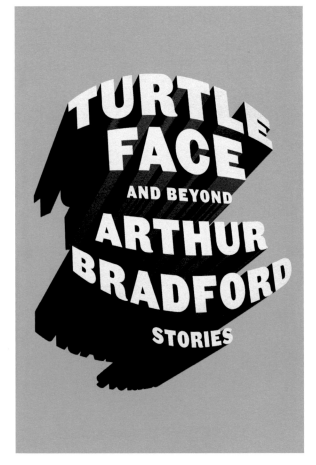

Jim Tierney

Jim Tierney grew up in rural Pennsylvania, and studied illustration at the University of the Arts in Philadelphia. He designed book covers at Penguin for several years after graduation, and currently works as a freelance illustrator/designer in Brooklyn, New York.

The Designer's Approach: I usually begin each job by sketching out a bunch of quick, tiny thumbnails. On average, it takes about ten thumbnails to come up with one decent idea, and once I have five or six of those, I'll work them up into color sketches for the art director. After that, it's just a matter of refining and tweaking the sketches until we find the right solution to finalize.

Although my work is mostly digital, I usually try to make as many things by hand as possible. Whether that means piecing together scanned drawings in Photoshop, or lettering directly onto a Cintiq tablet, I think retaining those personal imperfections is important to the charm and personality of my designs.

Pg 130, top left: The Lakeside Press, Art direction: Erica Heisman; top right: Viking, Art direction: Paul Buckley; bottom left: Penguin, Art direction: Roseanne Serra, Paul Buckley; bottom right: Picador, Art direction: Henry Sene Yee | Pg 131, top left: Viking, Art direction: Paul Buckley; top right: Penguin, Art direction: Paul Buckley; bottom left: Viking, Art direction: Paul Buckley; bottom right: Head of Zeus, Art direction: Laura Palmer | Pg 132, top left: Penguin, Art direction: Roseanne Serra, Paul Buckley; top right: Ecco, Art direction: Allison Saltzman; bottom left: Harper Collins, Art direction: Lucy Ruth Cummins; bottom right: St. Martin's Press, Art direction: Olga Grlic

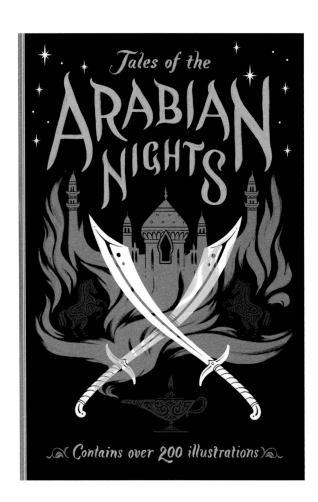

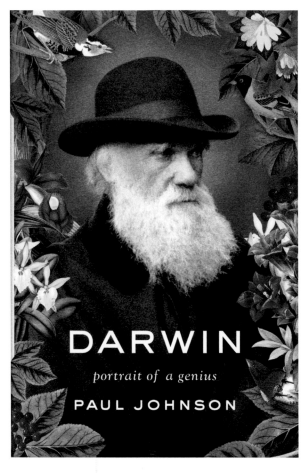

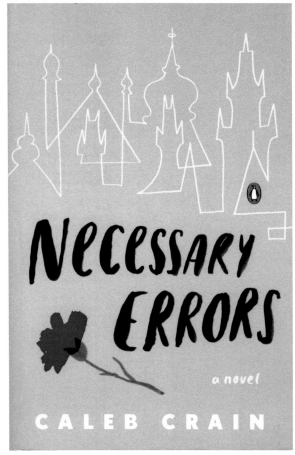

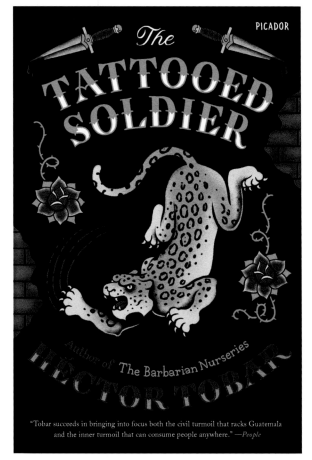

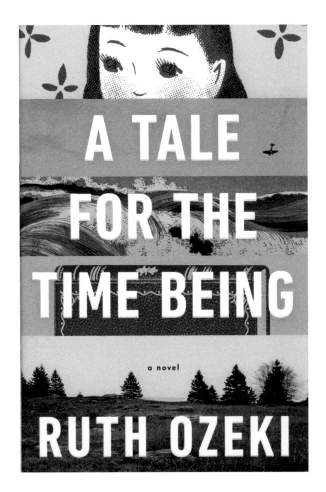

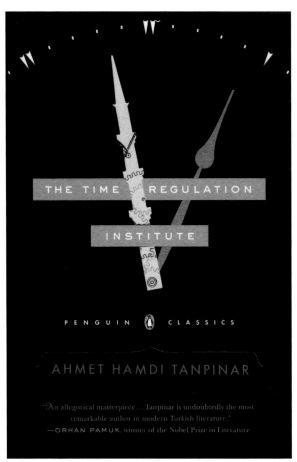

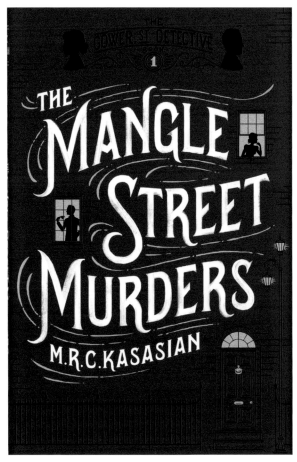

a life

by EDNA O'BRIEN

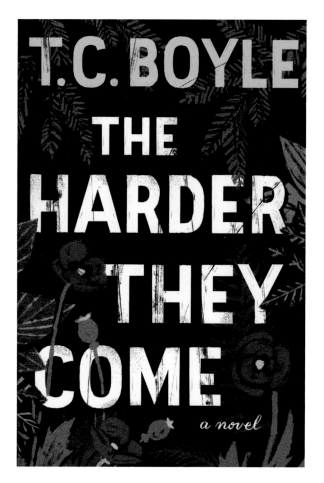

T.C. BOYLE

THE HARDER THEY COME

a novel

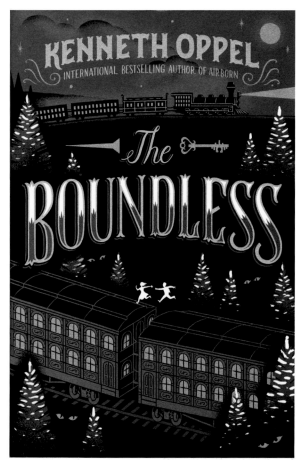

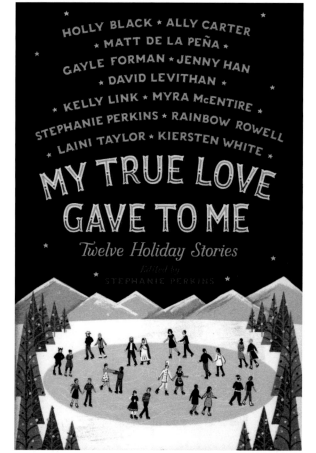

Kimberly Glyder

Kimberly Glyder is currently principal at Kimberly Glyder Design, a design firm based in the Philadelphia area. Her book design has been recognized with numerous awards, including the AIGA "50 Books/50 Covers" show. A graduate of the Rhode Island School of Design, Kimberly has given lectures at various colleges and museums on the topic of book cover design.

The Designer's Approach: A cover design always begins with the writing. I start by reading the manuscript, then distilling the major themes, and finally sketching out concepts. From there I go on to image research (either photography or illustration), though sometimes I create my own lettering or illustration depending on what is needed for a design.

My goal is to create an evocative cover to the book, something that suggests the major themes or characters. As designers, we're trying to get book buyers to pick up a book in a store or "click" on the book online. What may work as a literal interpretation of the writing is sometimes not commercially viable. Hopefully, the end product is one that is visually appealing, conceptual, and engaging.

Pg 134, top left: W. W. Norton; top right: Graywolf Press, Cover photos: New York Public Library (top) / George Marks, Retrofile RF; bottom left: Soho Press, Image © Lynea, engraving: C.Delon; bottom right: Soho Press I Pg 135: Vintage Books I Pg 136, top left: Random House; top right: Random House; bottom left: University of Nevada Press; bottom right: Graywolf Press, Painting (screened back): Mario Bachelli

THE
KING

poems

REBECCA WOLFF

THE CONVERT
A TALE OF EXILE AND EXTREMISM
DEBORAH BAKER

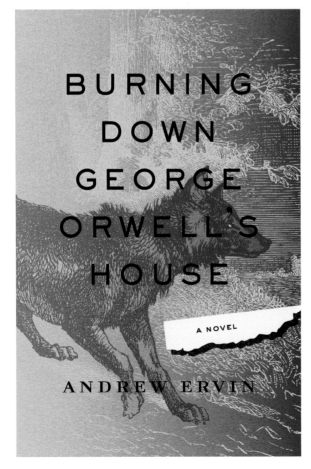

BURNING
DOWN
GEORGE
ORWELL'S
HOUSE

A NOVEL

ANDREW ERVIN

"The spirits of Oscar Wilde and Evelyn Waugh glower benignly over this very funny first novel."
—*The New York Times*

THE *Liar*

A Novel

STEPHEN FRY

THE COLOR OF NIGHT

"A truly unnerving mythical novel that asks us to piece together what is left of a shattered collective unconscious. Bell's devastated, traumatized characters surf the debris of who we are and where we've been." —A.M.Homes, author of *This Book Will Save Your Life*

Madison Smartt Bell

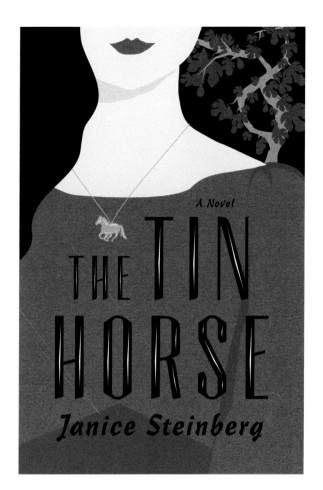

A Novel

THE TIN HORSE

Janice Steinberg

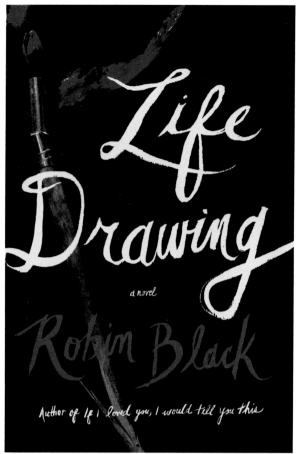

Life Drawing

a novel

Robin Black

Author of If I loved you, I would tell you this

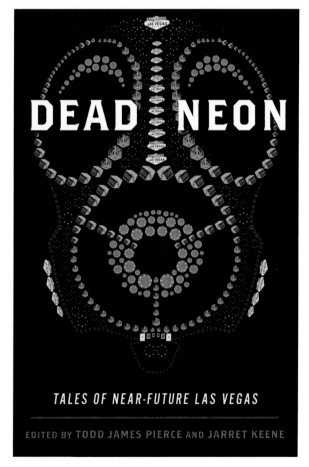

DEAD NEON

TALES OF NEAR-FUTURE LAS VEGAS

EDITED BY TODD JAMES PIERCE AND JARRET KEENE

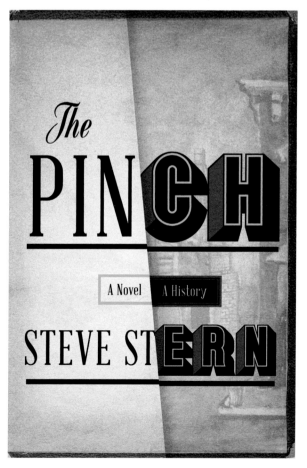

The PINCH

A Novel   A History

STEVE STERN

Kirk DouPonce

Kirk DouPonce has had the privilege of designing book covers for twenty years now. His career started as a freelancer right out of college. He was able to pick up a few jobs here and there, including book covers; but, for the most part, it was the National Guard that paid his rent. A couple of years later, Kirk made the difficult but correct choice of becoming an employee. Two of the companies he worked for were publishers. Being an in-house designer taught him so much more than he could have learned on his own. He now has a fuller understanding of the publishing and print industries. Later, David Uttley, a successful designer whose work Kirk greatly admired, asked him to hire on with him. Together they started what is now Faceout Studio, a firm known for designing exceptional book covers. More than anywhere else it was there that Kirk learned how to design under pressure. David and he were each designing over a hundred covers a year and the pace wasn't slowing down. To share the load, David gradually hired more designers and administrators. After many years, Kirk felt it was time to go back to his dream job of freelancing. That's when he and his wife started DogEared Design.

The Designer's Approach: My process for creating covers has changed a bit over the years. Each project still begins with lots of coffee and research, but now I like to create my own imagery instead of relying on stock sites, photographers, and illustrators. With the help of YouTube and a plethora of other tutorial sites, I've been able to teach myself photography and 3D. Considering how much I had been paying out for these services, it didn't take long to justify purchasing and learning these tools. What surprised me was how much I enjoy using them. My goal is to eventually be able to create "anything." If a client says they want an Amish vampire riding a steampunk dragon in outer space, I'd like to be able to say, "Sure, I can do that." After all these years, I'm still a student . . . and will always be one.

Pg 138: Thomas Nelson, Inc., Art director: Julie Faires | Pg 139, top left: Wiley, Art director: Adrian Morgan; top right: SourceBooks, Illustration: Milt Klingensmith, Art director: Greg Avila; bottom left: B&H Publishing Group, Art director: Diana Lawrence; bottom right: B&H Publishing Group, Art director: Diana Lawrence | Pg 140, top left: Orbit Books, Art director: Lauren Panepinto; top right: Moody Publishers, Art director: Judy Tollberg; bottom left: Brazos Press / Baker Publishing Group, Art Director: Paula Gibson; bottom right: Harper Collins / Blink, Art Director: Deborah Washburn

WHEN GROWTH STALLS

The Seven Reasons It Happens and a
Perscription for What to Do About It

Steve McKee

with Karl Weber

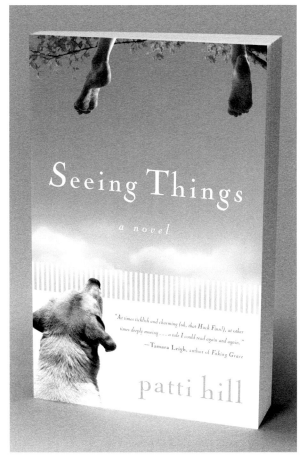

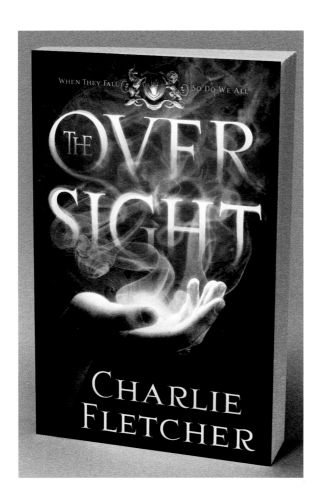

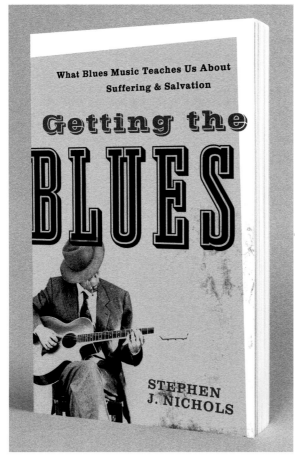

Mark Melnick

Mark Melnick has been a freelance graphic designer in New York City since 2002. Prior to that, he worked at Vintage Books (a division of Penguin Random House), Viking Books (also a division of Penguin Random House), was a design assistant at M&Co, and an intern at *Interview* and *Art in America* magazines. He also attended College of Wooster, in Wooster, Ohio.

The Designer's Approach: My approach is to read whatever material I'm given, and whatever related material I can dig up. I get as much information from the art director/editor as I can and do as much picture research as possible. I do as much sketching as I can. Then I synthesize all of the above into a cover that captures both the content and the tone of the text. Repeat.

Pg 142, top left: Theatre Communications Group, Photograph: Paula Court; top right: Farrar, Straus and Giroux, Photograph: Blake Gordon; bottom: W. W. Norton & Company, Photograph: Richard Kolker | Pg 143, top: Riverhead Books, Photograph: Michael Blann; bottom left: Scientific American / Farrar, Straus and Giroux; bottom right: Theatre Communications Group, Photograph: Mark Weiss | Pg 144, top left: W. W. Norton & Company, Brooke portrait: Josh Neufeld; top right: Liveright; bottom left: W. W. Norton & Company; bottom right: W. W. Norton & Company

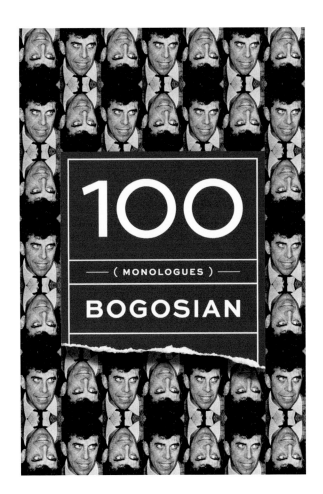

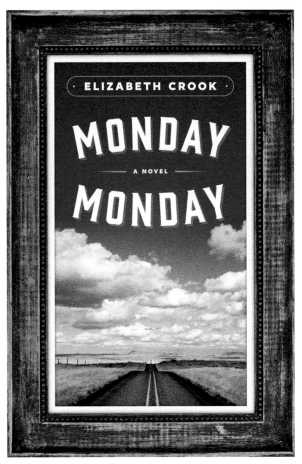

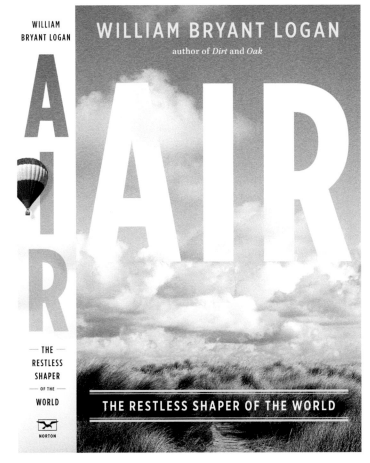

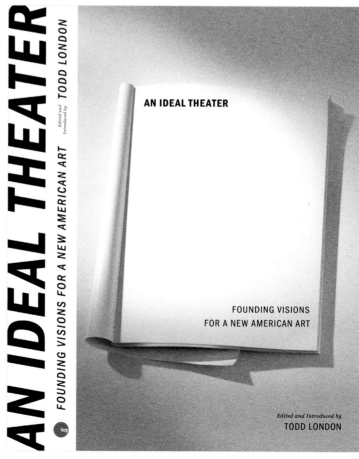

THE
INFLUENCING MACHINE

BROOKE GLADSTONE ON THE MEDIA

ILLUSTRATED BY JOSH NEUFELD

KINGDOM COME

A NOVEL

J.G. BALLARD

"J.G. Ballard is the undisputed laureate of suburban psychosis . . . a brilliant novel." —THE LITERARY REVIEW

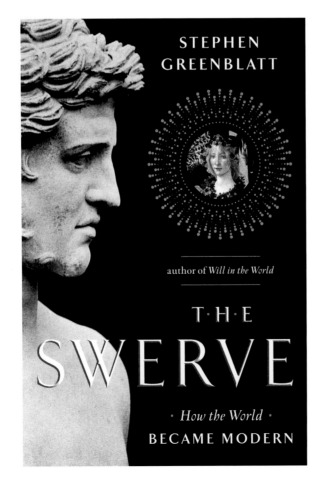

STEPHEN
GREENBLATT

author of *Will in the World*

T·H·E
SWERVE

· How the World ·
BECAME MODERN

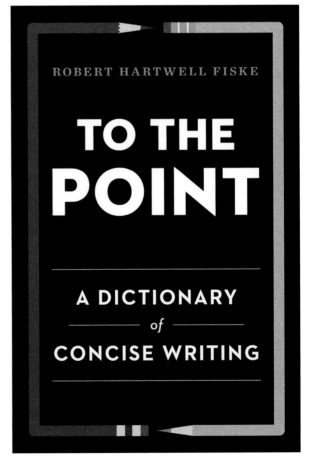

ROBERT HARTWELL FISKE

TO THE
POINT

A DICTIONARY
of
CONCISE WRITING

Matt Avery

Matt Avery is principal designer at the University of Chicago Press where he has been working since 2003. His work has been recognized by the Type Director's Club, the Chicago Design Museum, AIGA's "50 books/50 covers," *Communication Arts Typography Annual*, *Print*, STA, AAUP, and the Chicago Book Clinic.

The Designer's Approach: A good book cover for a nonfiction title (where the bulk of my experience lies) does two things well. First, it tells you in some fashion, to a greater or lesser degree, what the book is about. This is the editorial component of a book cover. Even (or perhaps especially) for the more esoteric subjects I work with, I find it's the more succinct approach to this editorial aspect that is most successful. An extreme example would be the typographic cover where the title really speaks for itself and where the typography might merely lend the title inflection—or not. The second thing a book cover should do is persuade the prospective reader to pick it up and take it home. This is the marketing/sales component. Toward that end, the book cover need not necessarily be attractive (although that is often the case), but it should be compelling. Hopefully, the editorial and marketing aspects will lead naturally one into the other, but at times they are in greater tension. At the end of the day, the goal of a cover is to connect the book with its natural audience and to make that audience as wide as possible.

My cover design process begins with a launch meeting with the publisher. Any suggestions from the author are aired, and we briefly discuss a possible strategy for approaching the cover. From there, the stages are as follows: reading, research, brainstorming, and layout. You might be disappointed to know that for nonfiction titles I do not usually read the entire text. (A work of fiction needs to be approached as the work of art that it is and considered in its totality.) For a nonfiction title, the designer needs to have a grasp of the central argument being put forth. I read the editorial statement and then as much of the manuscript as I need to. Often reading the introduction and conclusion suffices. For research, I will look at any other titles the author has published, other similar books (to avoid well-trod ground), then perhaps some preliminary image research to scare out a visual hook or inspiration. Along the way, I'm jotting down ideas in the form of words and sketches. Following that, I will brainstorm, during which I focus to come up with as many ideas as possible. The most promising idea(s) from this stage I will use to make actual layouts. Whether or not the layouts seem to be coming together well or not, at some point I run out of either energy or time and put them aside. Viewing the layouts the next day with fresh eyes, I can tell right away whether or not my layouts are working at all, the minor problems now being painfully obvious. If you don't have the luxury of time, show your layout to a trusted colleague. There are many ways, from A to Z, and sometimes steps are skipped or fall in a different order.

Pg 146: Photograph, Kristen Avery | Pg 146-148, all covers: The University of Chicago Press

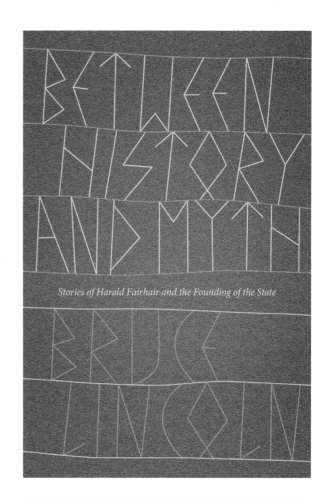

BAS JAN ADER

———

DEATH IS
ELSEWHERE

Alexander Dumbadze

BETWEEN
HISTORY
AND MYTH

Stories of Harald Fairhair and the Founding of the State

BRUCE
LINCOLN

LAWRENCE B. GLICKMAN
BUYING
POWER
A HISTORY OF
CONSUMER
ACTIVISM
IN AMERICA

The Atheist's Bible

THE MOST
DANGEROUS BOOK
THAT
NEVER EXISTED

Georges Minois

TRANSLATED BY LYS ANN WEISS

A Biography   Dominic A. Pacyga

CHICAGO

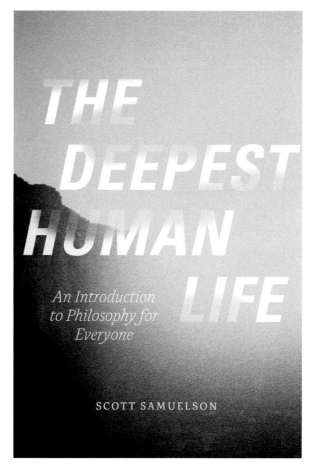

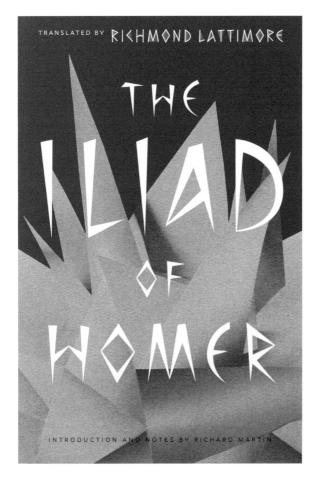

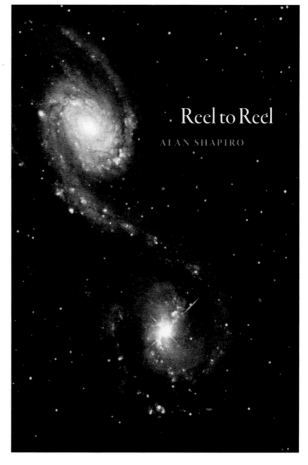

Matt Dorfman

Matt Dorfman is a designer, illustrator, and art director of *The New York Times*' Op/Ed page.

The Designer's Approach: I've worked on book covers that didn't have manuscripts available to read in advance. It's not my preferred process. Attempting a cover without reading the book is the design equivalent of trying to find a restroom in a hotel corridor with no light while tripping over a stack of upright folding chairs. So reading is pretty important.

I pick apart the author's delivery slightly more than I do the actual story. My favorite writers tend to manicure their voices from book to book in order to serve their story's reason to exist. When I'm designing, I'm minding that story's meaning and intent, but what I'm really trying to do is to resolve what that voice might look like. In an ideal circumstance, I'm hunting for a visual experience that can interest a total stranger in the book without over-explaining the particulars. If the author and I have both done our jobs, the cover gets ignored throughout most of the reader's trek through however many hundreds of pages the book may be, and when they come out on the other side having finished it, they should have a more personal perspective on what the cover might mean.

This alchemy is accomplished by reading the manuscript as many times as I can, scribbling very fast, very crude drawings in my sketchbook, and slamming my head in a drawer until I arrive at ideas that feel instinctively appropriate. This is not the same thing as something *looking* appropriate. They're separate concerns—both of which are important—but I'm preoccupied with how a design feels before I judge how it looks.

Pg 150, top left: Viking; top right: Softskull; bottom left: Anchor; bottom right: Verso I Pg 151: Riverhead I Pg 152: Softskull I Pg 153, top left: Penguin Press; top right: Pantheon; bottom left: Pantheon; bottom right: Anchor

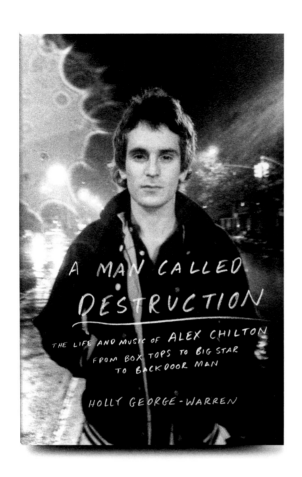

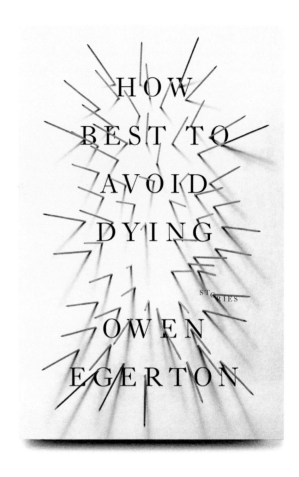

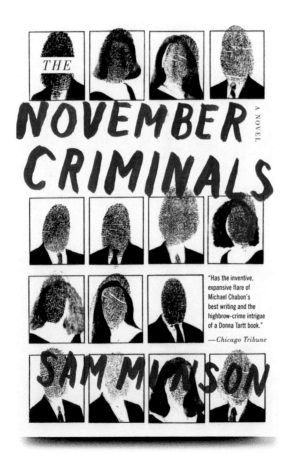

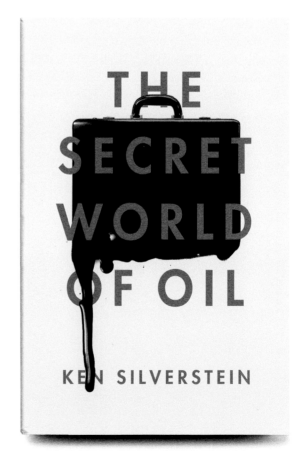

THE
PSYCHOPATH
TEST

A
JOURNEY
THROUGH
THE
MADNESS
INDUSTRY

JON RONSON

BESTSELLING AUTHOR OF *THEM* AND
THE MEN WHO STARE AT GOATS

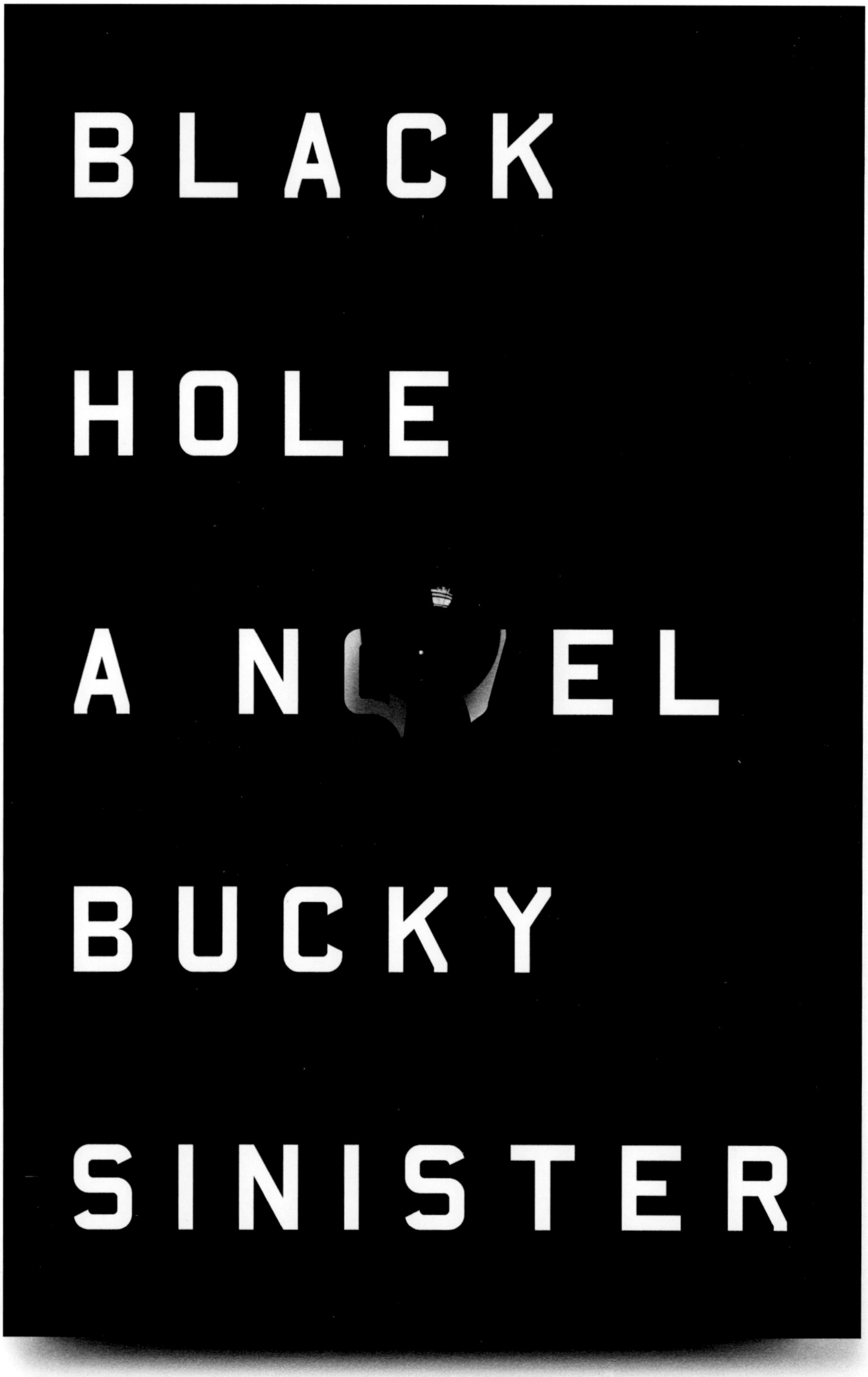
BLACK
HOLE
A NOVEL
BUCKY
SINISTER

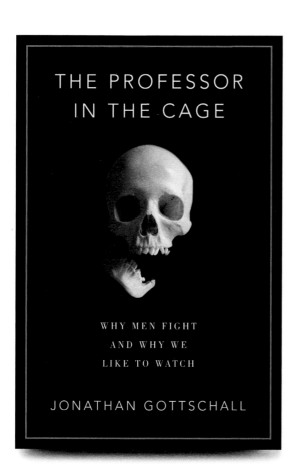

THE PROFESSOR
IN THE CAGE

WHY MEN FIGHT
AND WHY WE
LIKE TO WATCH

JONATHAN GOTTSCHALL

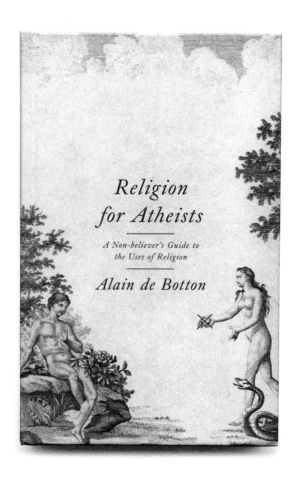

*Religion
for Atheists*

*A Non-believer's Guide to
the Uses of Religion*

Alain de Botton

*Religion
for Atheists*

*A Non-believer's Guide to
the Uses of Religion*

Alain de Botton

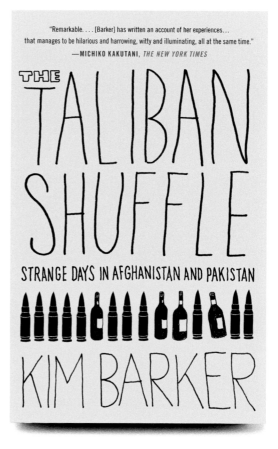

"Remarkable. . . . [Barker] has written an account of her experiences…
that manages to be hilarious and harrowing, witty and illuminating, all at the same time."
—MICHIKO KAKUTANI, *THE NEW YORK TIMES*

THE
TALIBAN
SHUFFLE

STRANGE DAYS IN AFGHANISTAN AND PAKISTAN

KIM BARKER

Melissa Gerber

Melissa Gerber grew up in Rochester, New York and is a graduate of the Rochester Institute of Technology. Her career started in New York City with a small packaging firm, but then she moved into publishing, working for Penguin Group USA and then Running Press Book Publishers in Philadelphia. She was offered a position of Associate Art Director at Sterling Publishing and managed titles there for four years. Deciding to focus purely on design, she left to become a freelance designer and now works with clients across the country from her studio in Wilmington, Delaware.

The Designer's Approach: I see each cover design as a brand new work of art to create. Inspiration can strike at any moment, so when I spot something that inspires me, I tuck it away in my mind for future use. I prefer a more timeless look, with small pops of current trends. With most of the covers I design, they have to be youthful and stylish, but it is important to create a great classic piece without selling out with every popular trend at once. It also needs to reflect the content within the book. Every time I sit down at my computer to begin a new cover there is a surge of excitement, not knowing what the design will become.

My process of designing always begins with the client's needs. I take into consideration the trim size, the target audience, the budget, as well as any design vision the publisher may have. Additionally, I research the competition to see what is already on the market so I can begin every cover with a fresh approach. As I begin a new project, I start with three to four completely different ideas. I like to make sure the client has safer, more conservative concepts as well as anything they specifically requested. Then I go beyond the expected, with more compelling designs. I understand that in some cases the client has firm expectations of how the cover should look, but that won't stop me from throwing in something unexpected. You never know when the publisher will fall in love with something they never knew they wanted. As I work out those initial concepts, my mind gets pulled from one idea to another and in the end I may have twenty different options for one cover project. This may seem extreme, but it is a great place to work from. I will then go through them once more and remove any options that aren't as strong as I'd like, sending the rest for a first review. By giving more then a few ideas early on it gives the client and I some nice talking points. I always want to make sure that the publisher can see the effort I put into every design I send. They should know that their cover is special and that I have put all of my energy into creating an innovative design for their product. In the first round of cover options I may have given them an idea that they absolutely love and decide to use, but I am also not afraid to admit that I have had to start over on more than one occasion.

Sometimes there isn't time to brainstorm as many ideas as I would like. In the past, I have had a publisher walk into my office or send me a note saying they need a cover design ready for a meeting in thirty minutes. Instances like this have taught me how to work under pressure. I let my creativity flow with whatever concepts come to me first and pump ideas out quickly and efficiently. Although stressful, I am thankful for situations like this because it helps to sharpen my design and problem-solving skills, creating a sense of confidence in myself.

Pg 155, top: Charlesbridge Publishing, Inc.; bottom left: Running Press Book Publishers; bottom right: Charlesbridge Publishing, Inc. | Pg 156, top left: Charlesbridge Publishing, Inc.; top right: Charlesbridge Publishing, Inc.; bottom left: Charlesbridge Publishing, Inc.; bottom right: Imagine Publishing | Pg 157, top: Charlesbridge Publishing, Inc.; bottom left: Penguin Group (USA); bottom right: Charlesbridge Publishing, Inc.

ORGANIC
SWEETS and TREATS
More than 70 Delicious Recipes
Michal Moses & Ivana Nitzan

CANDY
Cocktails
FUN AND FLIRTY DRINKS
WITH A *Sugar-Kissed* TWIST
FLANNERY GOOD AND KATHERINE GOOD

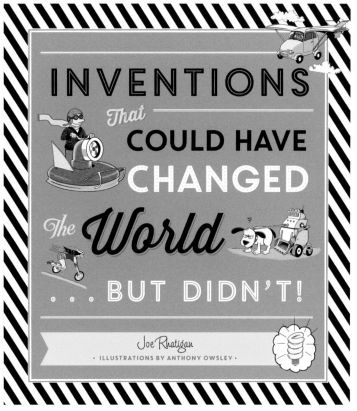

INVENTIONS
That COULD HAVE
CHANGED
The World
.... BUT DIDN'T!
Joe Rhatigan
ILLUSTRATIONS BY ANTHONY OWSLEY

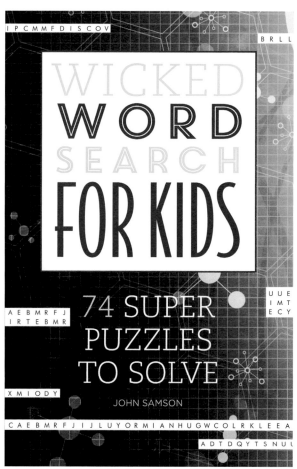

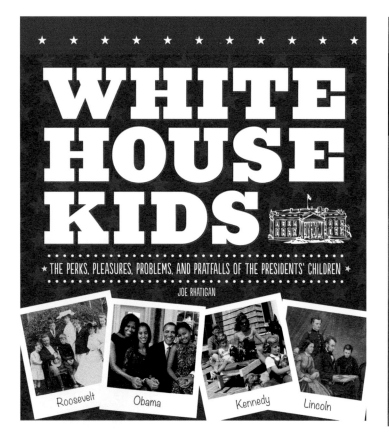

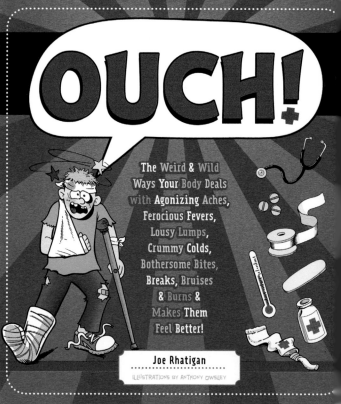

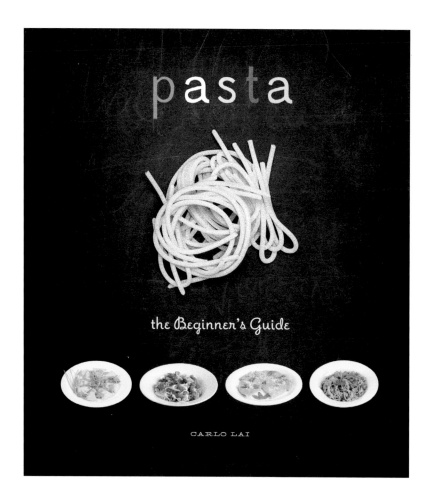

pasta

the Beginner's Guide

CARLO LAI

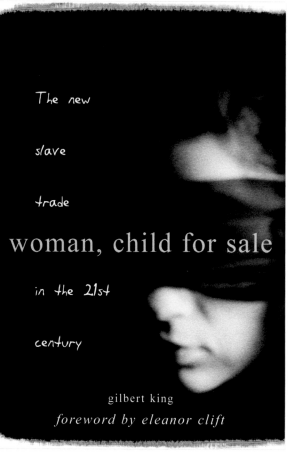

The new

slave

trade

woman, child for sale

in the 21st

century

gilbert king

foreword by eleanor clift

THE ART OF

DECEPTION

ILLUSIONS TO CHALLENGE THE EYE AND THE MIND

BRAD HONEYCUTT

FOREWORD BY JOHN LANGDON
EPILOGUE BY SCOTT KIM

Michael Kellner

An ardent and constant reader since childhood, a former clerk in bookshops specializing in rare and out-of-print books, a magazine designer and art director for more than twenty years, **Michael Kellner** has been designing book covers and jackets, when given the chance, since 1996. His work has won Anthony Awards for cover design from *The Anthony Boucher Memorial World Mystery Convention*, and has been recognized by *Print* magazine and *Graphic Design USA*.

The Designer's Approach: In a letter to his American publisher dated 1958, Kingsley Amis writes, "Please give the jacket artist my warm congratulations for a bright design that beautifully renders the spirit of the book." Reading this I thought: Exactly. Rendering the spirit of a book—strikingly, skillfully, artfully—is exactly what designers strive to do. Doing it well is the tricky part.

The best designs can result from sheer creative persistence. Sometimes they come about spontaneously, instances of supernal inspiration. Most times they're the product of a happy confluence of skill, talent, and luck. Skill benefits from experience; talent is mysterious even, or especially, to oneself; and luck is what you never want to be without.

Cover design is both an art and a service. It takes a long time and a lot of work to write and publish a book. Designers have a responsibility to the author, the editor, the publisher, and readers. Modesty compels remembering that a good book with a bad cover will always be read, while a bad book, even with a great cover, will never enjoy the same reward.

Pg 159, top left: Akashic Press; top right: Counterpoint Press, Cover photograph: Pieter Van Damme; bottom left: Counterpoint Press, Film still: private collection; bottom right: Busted Flush Press I Pg 160, left: Dennis McMillan Publications; right: Dennis McMillan Publications I Pg 161, top left: Dennis McMillan Publications, Original photography: Christopher Voelker, Illustration: Jenny Adams; top right: Dennis McMillan Publications, Original photography: Christopher Voelker; bottom left: Counterpoint Press, Front cover, lower right, detail of The Large Glass (1915–1923) by Marcel Duchamp © Philadelphia Museum of Art/ Corbis,© Estate of Marcel Duchamp/ADAGP, Paris; Author photo: Zoe Nicoladis; bottom right: Dennis McMillan Publications, Original photography: Christopher Voelker

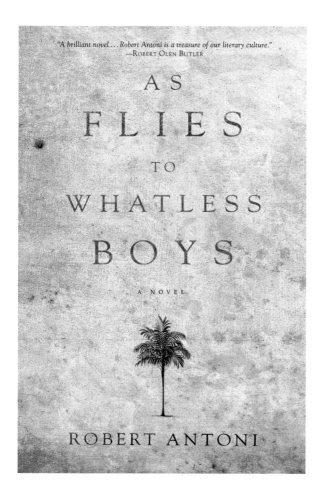

"A brilliant novel . . . Robert Antoni is a treasure of our literary culture."
—ROBERT OLEN BUTLER

AS
FLIES
TO
WHATLESS
BOYS

A NOVEL

ROBERT ANTONI

Cementville

a novel | Paulette Livers

The
Hackman
Blues

KEN
BRUEN

Award-winning author of **THE GUARDS** and **LONDON BOULEVARD**

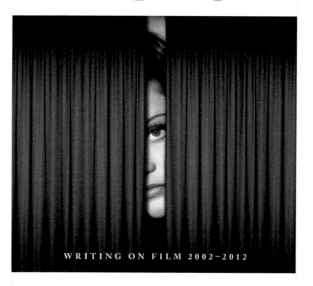

stolenglimpses

WRITING ON FILM 2002–2012

captiveshadows

GEOFFREY O'BRIEN

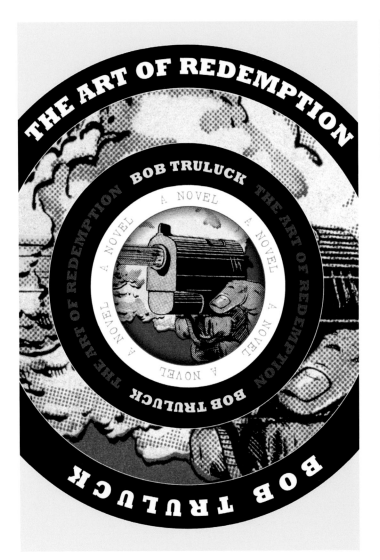

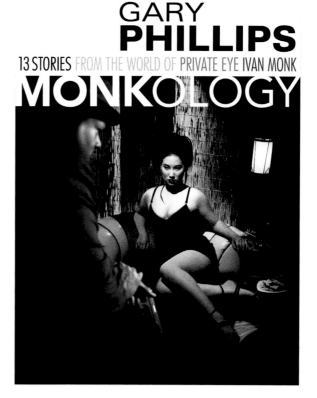

Natalie Olsen

Natalie Olsen is an observer; a question-asker; a juggler; an interpreter; a wanderer; a collector; a collager; a critic; a recycler; a presenter; a doodler; the owner of a company called Kisscut Design; a freelance book designer for various publishers across North America; the recipient of some flattering tweets, gifted bottles of scotch, and design awards; but first and foremost, a reader.

The Designer's Approach: My precise work flow depends on the practical constraints for each unique project. Things like genre, audience, budget, time frame, client requests, and the amount of caffeine I have consumed that day. But for the most part, I sit in a Herman Miller chair (you know the one) and traverse the needs of the publisher, the editor, the sales department, the author, the author's mom/kids/cat, and that voice in my head that pushes me to make good work (you know the one).

I gather information and inspiration from wherever I can—the creative brief, the manuscript, the shelves of my local bookstore, the streets of my neighborhood, the comparative titles with covers likely made by the accomplished designers in this book, an evening out with the author—and then produce the sum of it all in a rectangle that is approximately six inches wide by nine inches tall.

Throughout every stage, from the reading to the rejecting, I focus on the endurance of the cover concept: after it initially entices someone to pick it up, will it accompany them while they turn pages, and will it stay with them long after they finish reading, on a shelf, as a memento of the story?

Pg 163, top left: NeWest Press; top right: Athabasca University Press; bottom left: Freehand Books (an imprint of Broadview Press); bottom right: Freehand Books (an imprint of Broadview Press) | Pg 164, left: NeWest Press; right: ECW Press | Pg 165, top left: Playwrights Canada Press; top right: ECW Press; bottom left: NeWest Press; bottom right: ECW Press

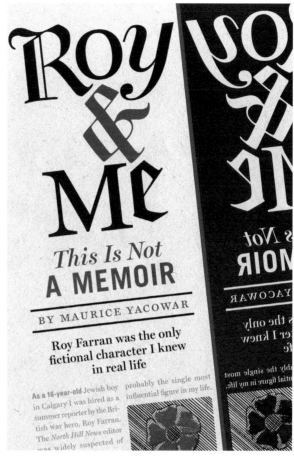

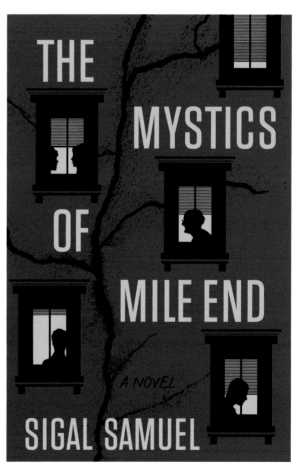

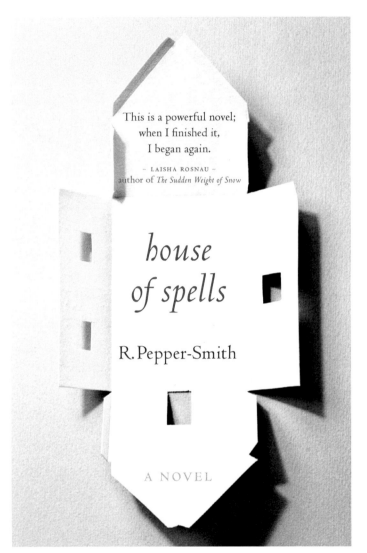

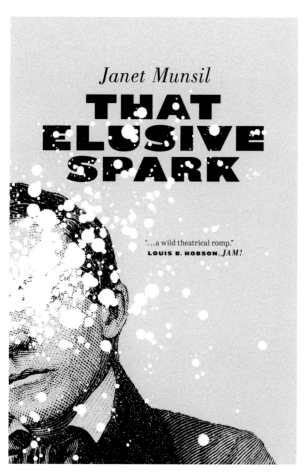

Janet Munsil

THAT ELUSIVE SPARK

"...a wild theatrical romp."
LOUIS B. HOBSON, *JAM!*

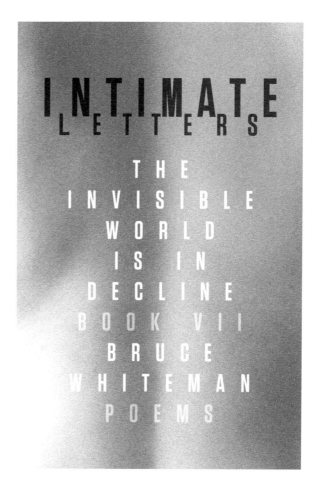

INTIMATE LETTERS

THE
INVISIBLE
WORLD
IS IN
DECLINE
BOOK VII
BRUCE
WHITEMAN
POEMS

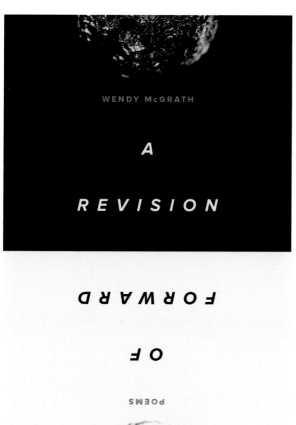

WENDY McGRATH

A

REVISION

FORWARD

OF

POEMS

POEMS
SUZANNAH SHOWLER

Natalie F. Smith

Natalie F. Smith is currently a book designer at Duke University Press. Previously, she was an in-house book designer at the University of Chicago Press. Natalie grew up in Louisiana and began her career in book design with an internship at Louisiana State University Press. Her cover designs have been recognized by AIGA, *Print,* the Society of Typographic Arts, *Communication Arts*, and the American Association of University Presses.

The Designer's Approach: I begin with research and review of the book materials provided by the publisher and I quickly generate ideas. Then, I forget about most—or all—of the ideas and open a blank page with nothing but the title. I focus on what the title alone communicates and obsess over how to clarify and amplify the message. I look for connections and try to draw links from themes of the book to familiar symbols. I'll knead, carve, add, and subtract until the design solution seems to be both simple and (I hope) surprising.

Pg 166: Courtesy of Ivan Weiss | Pg 167, top left: The University of Chicago Press, Art director: Jill Shimabukuro; top right: The University of Chicago Press, Cover photograph: Beverly Joubert / National Geographic Stock, Art director: Jill Shimabukuro; bottom left: The University of Chicago Press, Art director: Jill Shimabukuro; bottom right: The University of Chicago Press, Art director: Jill Shimabukuro, (*unpublished cover design at time of printing) | Pg 168, left: The University of Chicago Press, Cover photograph: Weegee (Arthur Fellig), Warming Up (ca. 1938), International Center of Photography, Art director: Jill Shimabukuro; right: The University of Chicago Press, Art director: Jill Shimabukuro | Pg 169, left: The University of Chicago Press, Art director: Jill Shimabukuro; right: The University of Chicago Press, Cover photograph: Matt Avery, Art director: Jill Shimabukuro

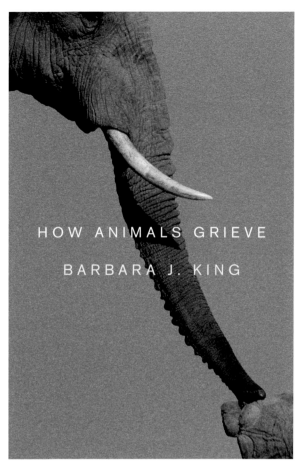

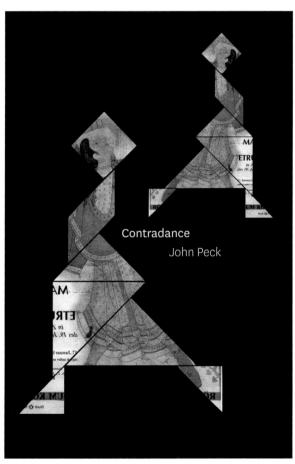

INFIDEL
POETICS

RIDDLES, NIGHTLIFE, SUBSTANCE

DANIEL TIFFANY

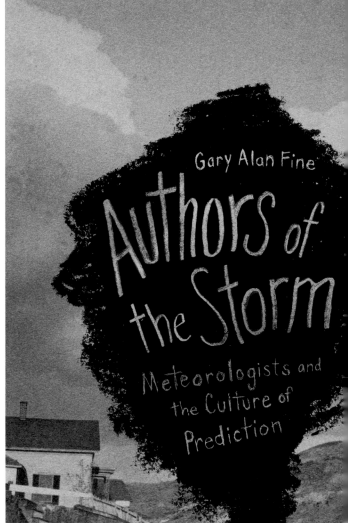

Gary Alan Fine

Authors of
the Storm

Meteorologists and
the Culture of
Prediction

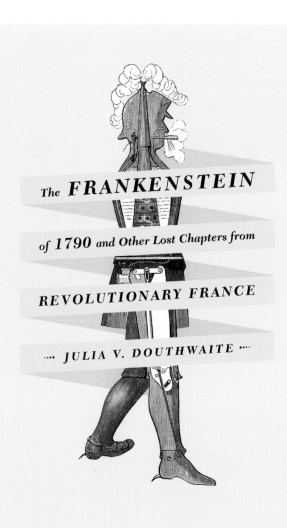

The FRANKENSTEIN

of 1790 and Other Lost Chapters from

REVOLUTIONARY FRANCE

···· JULIA V. DOUTHWAITE ····

EGATIONAL CHUR

I BELONG TO
THIS BAND,
HALLELUJAH!

COMMUNITY, SPIRITUALITY,
& TRADITION AMONG
SACRED HARP SINGERS

LAURA CLAWSON

Nathan Burton

Nathan Burton is a freelance designer based in London. He started his career as an in-house designer at Bloomsbury Publishing followed by a move to Penguin Books, working mainly on the Hamish Hamilton imprint. He left Penguin in 2008 to start up Nathan Burton Design.

The Designer's Approach: Here are a few things I like to keep in the back of my mind when designing a new book cover: It's helpful to have an understanding of genre and markets of publishing, but don't feel you always have to adhere to the "rules" of that genre. Briefs can be flexible, so don't be afraid of suggesting alternatives, but also know when to stick to the brief. Keep it simple, a well-executed simple idea can be much more effective than an overcomplicated design. Don't be afraid of clichés, but make sure its done in a new way. Make it attractive. Try to come up with a good idea rather than follow the current trends of design. When all that fails make the type big.

Pg 171, top left: Penguin; top right: Serpent's Tale; bottom left: Daunt Books; bottom right: JPushkin Press | Pg 172, top left: Quercus; top right: Quercus; bottom left: Quercus; bottom right: Penguin | Pg 173, left: Little, Brown, Photography: Shadi Ghadirian; right: Short Books

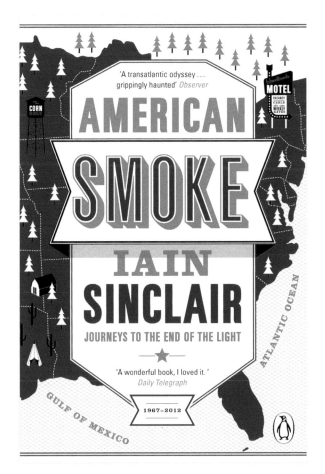

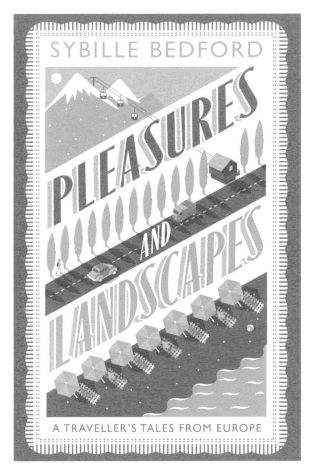

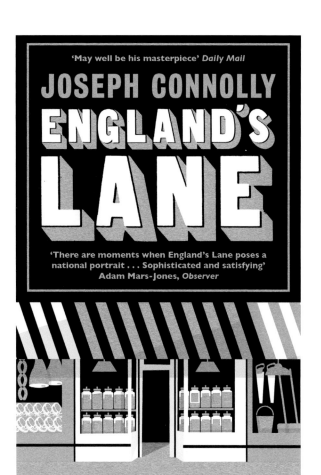

'May well be his masterpiece' *Daily Mail*

JOSEPH CONNOLLY
ENGLAND'S LANE

'There are moments when England's Lane poses a national portrait . . . Sophisticated and satisfying' Adam Mars-Jones, *Observer*

From the bestselling author of *England's Lane*

JOSEPH CONNOLLY
WINTER BREAKS

'They are a wild and unruly lot, these characters . . . fans of Connolly's will be delighted' *The Times*

JOSEPH CONNOLLY
THIS IS IT

'A jet black comedy . . . waspish, morose, neatly crafted and distressingly funny' *New Statesman*

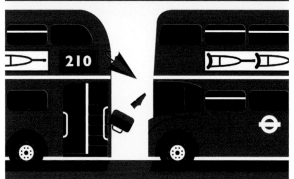

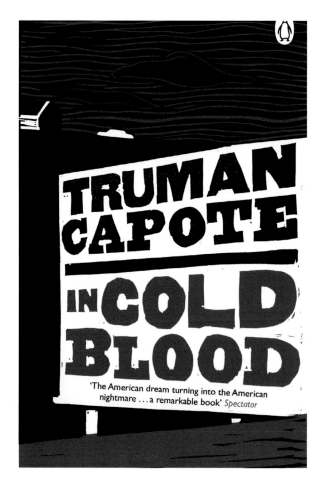

TRUMAN CAPOTE
IN COLD BLOOD

'The American dream turning into the American nightmare . . . a remarkable book' *Spectator*

Nicole Caputo

Nicole Caputo is an award-winning New York graphic designer with over a decade of experience specializing in book and book cover design. Her clients range from small independent presses to large commercial publishing houses, boutique hotels to independent authors. She is the VP, Creative Director, at Basic Books and has been a guest speaker at the NYU Center for Publishing. Her work has been published in *Graphic Design Solutions*, 5th Edition as well as other prestigious publications, including *Communication Arts*, *HOW* magazine, *Print* magazine, and the Type Director's Club and Art Director's Club annuals. Awards include the One Show, AIGA/ NY, HOW International Design, PRINT Regional Design, the New York Book Show, the National Gold Ink Awards, London International Creative Competition, Communication Arts, Type Director's Club, Art Director's Club, STEP Design Magazine, and the Publishing Professionals Network.

The Designer's Approach: It is important for me, as a designer, to be present and observant during my day-to-day life so that I can absorb ideas from many different sources: books, objects and events I notice on the street, in nature, or on the subway—the wonderful and the horrible alike. In this respect, my work is a seamless part of my life, and this early part of the process definitely informs my covers in interesting and unpredictable ways. Sometimes I will realize after I have completed a design, that something subconscious has been triggered, almost to the extent that I don't feel like I can take credit. I value that ongoing inspired thinking that begins before I open up the manuscript as a vital part of my process.

Once I have the manuscript, I prefer to read it through in its entirety. I always use printed pages and markup with pencil, dog-ear, connect portions, define words that may require defining, research. To sense the overall mood, I look for strong emotion and read very carefully and closely for details that may form a thread throughout and non-obvious striking visual cues within the text. When I start to design I often have several ideas and try to follow through with each one. Often they take me to the next one or to something entirely unexpected, so I do not like to cut that process short.

When the schedule allows, I like to live with the covers for a bit so, for example I print them and post them at home over the surface of a large mirror behind my work space, or sometimes I hang them in the kitchen so I can take the overall design in during preparation of meals. I will often create a mock up and spend time with it at work or at home, making refinements and changes along the way. Ideally there will be one beautiful visual that can represent a few of the important ideas in the book, remaining simple while also suggestive and rich. I especially enjoy high-concept design, which invites the viewer to pause and then, with any luck move past the cover, explore further, and buy the book!

Pg 175, left: Basic Books, Cover photography: Michael Duva; right: Counterpoint Press I Pg 176, left: Basic Books; right: Basic Books I Pg 177, top left: Basic Books, Jacket photography: Carol Wood; top right: Basic Books, Cover photography: David Prince; bottom left: W. W. Norton, Art director: Albert Tang; bottom right: Picador, Art direction: Henry Sene Yee's

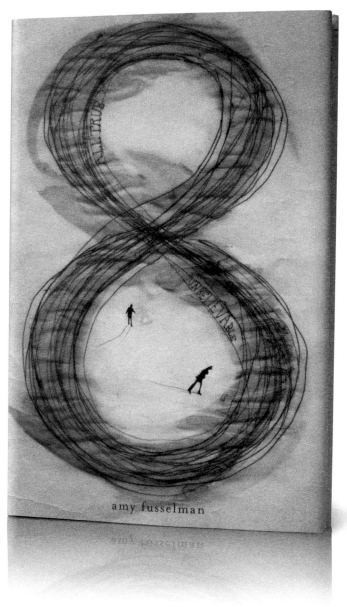

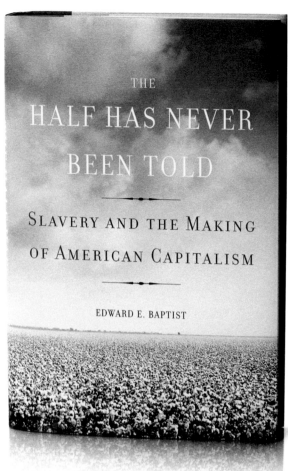

THE
HALF HAS NEVER
BEEN TOLD

SLAVERY AND THE MAKING
OF AMERICAN CAPITALISM

EDWARD E. BAPTIST

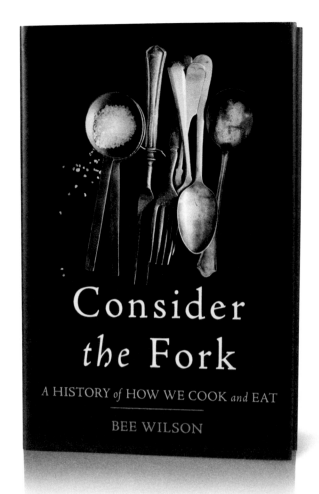

Consider
the Fork

A HISTORY of HOW WE COOK and EAT

BEE WILSON

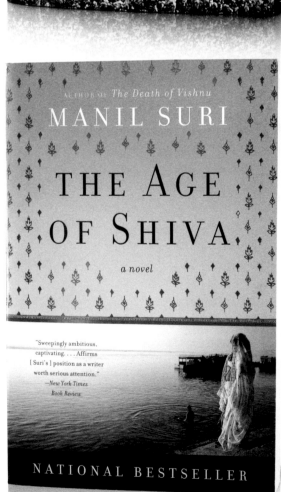

AUTHOR OF *The Death of Vishnu*
MANIL SURI
THE AGE
OF SHIVA
a novel

"Sweepingly ambitious,
captivating.... Affirms
[Suri's] position as a writer
worth serious attention."
—*New York Times
Book Review*

NATIONAL BESTSELLER

ALL for
Love
A NOVEL

DAN JACOBSON

PICADOR

Oliver Munday

Oliver Munday is a graphic designer living and working in New York City. His work has been recognized by many of the major design publications, including *Communication Arts*, TDC, *STEP inside Design* magazine's "25 freshest minds in design," *Young Guns 7*, AIGA "50 Books/50 Covers" and, in 2010, he was named one of *PRINT* magazine's "20 under 30," in the new visual artists review.

The Designer's Approach: My process when designing a book cover has evolved, and I imagine it will continue to evolve the more I read. I used to read a manuscript in search of an image to use, but this became a hindrance to my understanding of the text as a whole. I put too much pressure on making sure I didn't miss any potential imagery, and I was enjoying books less than when I was reading for pleasure. It felt more like work, and the stories left a cloudy imprint on my memory. I now approach it with less scrutiny and read the text with a greater sense of freedom. An idea might come to me a week after finishing. It might not be an image, either: it could be a feeling. I have allowed myself to become surprised by the process. This makes it exponentially more enjoyable as a reader.

Pg 179, all covers: Farrar, Straus & Giroux | Pg 180, top left: Farrar, Straus & Giroux/Scientific American; top right: Doubleday; bottom left: Farrar, Straus & Giroux; bottom right: Pantheon | Pg 181, top left: Riverhead; top right: Farrar, Straus & Giroux; bottom left: HarperCollins; bottom right: Knopf

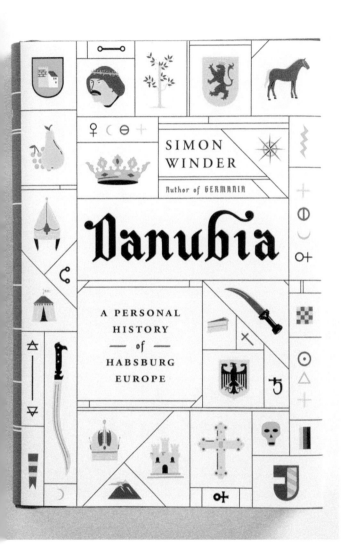

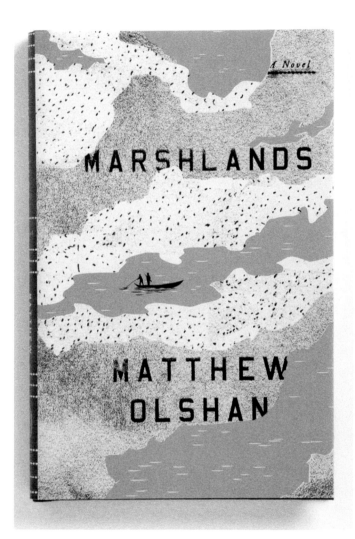

THE
IMPROBABILITY ◆
PRINCIPLE

WHY COINCIDENCES,
MIRACLES, AND ♠
RARE EVENTS
HAPPEN EVERY DAY ♥

DAVID J. HAND ♣

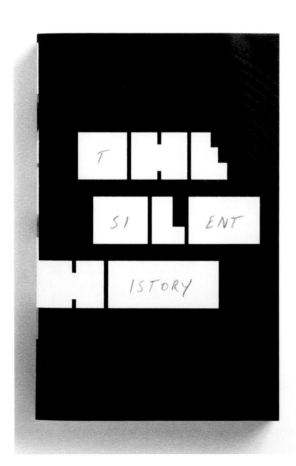

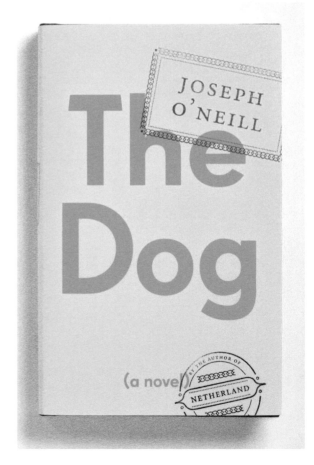

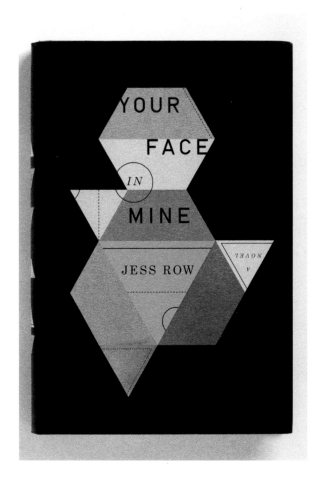

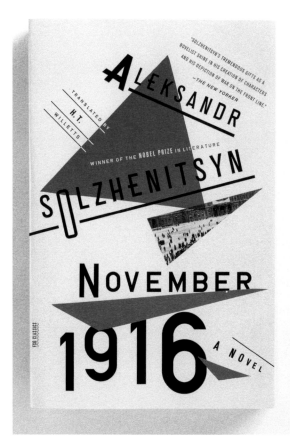

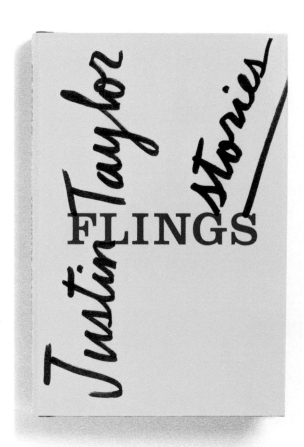

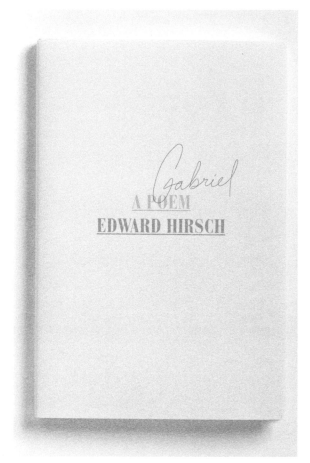

Paul Buckley

Paul Buckley is the vice president executive creative director at Penguin Random House/ Brooklyn Landlord.

The Designer's Approach: The needs of every book are different—therefore the way of approaching each cover is different every time. This is the fun and beauty of being a book designer and art director.

Pg 183, top left: Penguin; top right: Penguin, Art: Travis Louie; bottom: Penguin, Illustration: Noma Barr | Pg 184, top: Penguin Drop Caps series, Drop cap illustrations: Jessica Hische; bottom: Penguin Horror stories | Pg 185, all covers: Penguin, Black and white art: Vivienne Fleischer

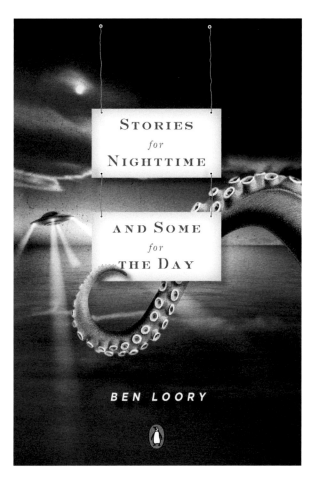

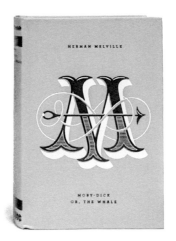

On The Road

KEROUAC

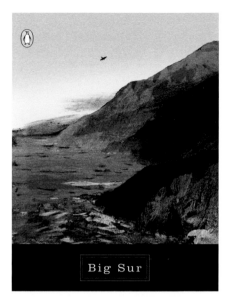

Big Sur

KEROUAC

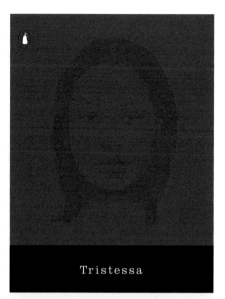

Tristessa

KEROUAC

Dharma Bums

KEROUAC

Visions of Cody

KEROUAC

Maggie Cassidy

KEROUAC

Rex Bonomelli

Rex Bonomelli is a graphic designer in Brooklyn, New York. Originally from Northern Virginia, he studied at the School of Visual Arts where he earned a BFA in graphic design. Rex worked as a designer at Red Herring Design and Spot Design, where he designed everything from CDs to theatrical advertising campaigns. He spent the next ten years in book publishing, serving as art director at Doubleday and Scribner, where he designed covers for authors as varied as Stephen King, Laura Bush, Don DeLillo, James Franco, Colm Tóibín, Jeannette Walls, and Bill O'Reilly. Rex has also worked at *The New York Times* Book Review and is currently the director of graphic design at the Metropolitan Opera.

The Designer's Approach: My design process is almost always the same. First, I start by reading the creative brief. This is always important because it is where you find out how the publisher sees the book and how they want to sell it. Often the designer's interpretation of a book is very different from the publisher's. Occasionally, I'll get a book that is supposed to be humorous, for instance, and then I'll read it and scratch my head wondering where the humor is. But as the designer, it's my job to listen to the client and not judge the product.

To help get a good overview of the publisher's expectations, I research the author's previous works and the comparable titles. I can usually get a sense of the boundaries of the design, or in some cases, what not to do. If a manuscript is available, I begin reading and taking notes. I often try to find visual elements in the text, or I look for meaningful moments that might illustrate the book in an unexpected way.

Then the real work begins. I'll often start with the most obvious solution just to get it out of my system. By going through this process, a smarter idea will often present itself. Some covers require me to do rounds and rounds of designs. Usually, these are the books that have a lot of expectations, so there are more people involved. My favorite books to work on are the under-the-radar books that don't have big names, or big numbers. I can usually get a good cover approved with these.

After I've designed a cover that's approved by the art director, it's out of my hands. The publisher, editor, author, sales and marketing team, and anyone else with a stake in the book get to have their say. Sometimes it goes well, and other times it's a disaster. I've sat in many sales meetings where a big book with a good cover got killed because everyone couldn't agree. What ultimately happens is the design gets compromised and no one is really happy. But in most cases, if I've done my job, the cover design gets approved and it's off into the world.

Pg 187, top: Scribner; bottom: Scribner | Pg 188, top left: New Directions, Art director: Rodrigo Corral; top right: Scribner; bottom left: New Harvest; bottom right: Scribner | Pg 189, top left: Scribner; top right: Scribner; bottom left: Simon and Schuster, Art director: Michael Accordino; bottom right: Liveright, Art director: Albert Tang.

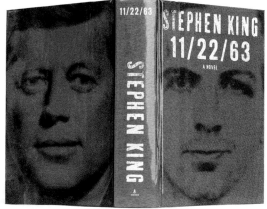

FOREWORD BY GREGORY MOSHER

EDITED, WITH AN INTRODUCTION, BY THOMAS KEITH

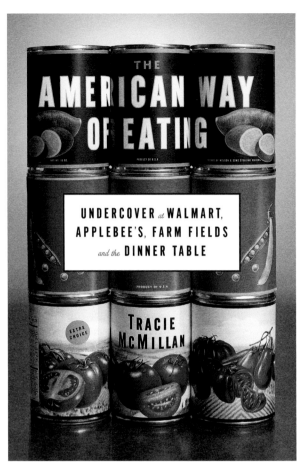

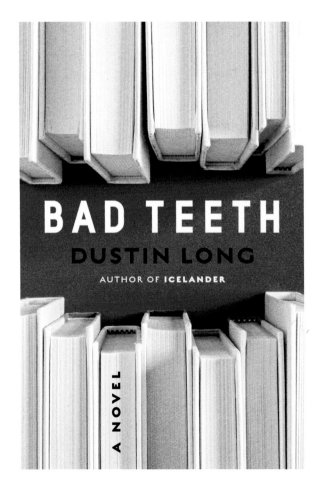

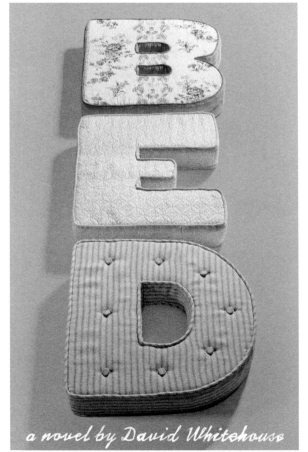

FROM SQUARE ONE

DEAN OLSHER

A Meditation, with Digressions, on Crosswords

1. Peer into their origins.

4. Ponder their purpose.

9. Witness the creation of an actual puzzle!

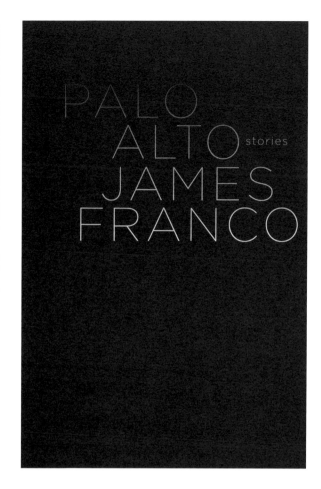

PALO ALTO stories JAMES FRANCO

PROMISE LAND

MY JOURNEY THROUGH AMERICA'S

→ SELF-HELP CULTURE ←

A MEMOIR BY

Jessica Lamb-Shapiro

THE DEATH OF IVAN ILYICH & A CONFESSION

LEO TOLSTOY

A NEW TRANSLATION BY PETER CARSON

INTRODUCTION BY MARY BEARD

Steve Attardo

Steve Attardo is the Art Director for Norton Paperbacks and Liveright as well as owner of Ninetynorth Design, a multidisciplinary design and illustration studio. His work has been recognized by the AIGA, *Print* magazine, New York Book Guild, *Complex* magazine, and he has been nominated for *Print* magazine's "20 under 30" award. Steve has twice been included in the AIGA/Design Observer's "50 books 50 covers" selection. When not working, he loves to run and loves to fly . . . preferably to an island with warm sand or a mountain with cold air.

The Designer's Approach: I don't feel my process is too rigid. I like to read and absorb the manuscript first while taking some notes and lists that don't usually make a ton of sense to an outsider. I'm trying to find the guts of the book. What is the right voice and what should the face of this story be? At times I'll start sketching thumbnails (which are also undecipherable to an outsider) to work through my ideas and other times I just like to dive in and start creating. Each project is a bit different, but once I start putting image and text on paper is when I really begin to navigate the ideas at hand and where the voice of the cover really takes shape. I don't stop until I feel the cover is communicating as clearly or as cryptically as it should. If I'm lucky, something I made was good enough to stick, so I can start refining and really crafting the end result. It's not a very unique way of working, but every project presents a new challenge to the process and each experience informs the next one in certain ways.

Pg 191, all covers: Ecco Books, Art director: Allison Saltzman | Pg 192, top left: Broadway, Art director: Jim Massey; top right: O/R Books; bottom left: Ecco Books, Art director: Allison Saltzman; bottom right: Algonquin, Art director: Anne Winslow | Pg 193, top left: Ecco Books, Art director: Allison Saltzman; top right: Ecco Books, Art director: Allison Saltzman; bottom left: O/R Books; bottom right: Ecco Books, Art director: Allison Saltzman | Pg 194, top: Ecco Books, Art director: Allison Saltzman; bottom: Sterling, Art director: Jo Obarowski

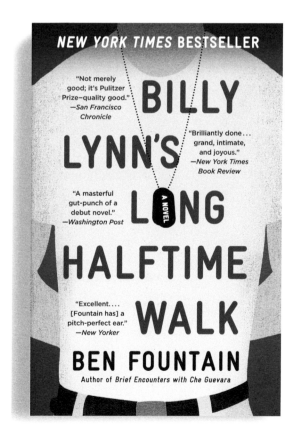

THE DAY
THE WORLD
ENDS
(POEMS)
ETHAN
COEN

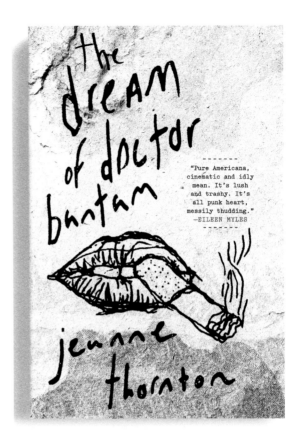

the
dream
of doctor
bantam

"Pure Americana,
cinematic and idly
mean. It's lush
and trashy. It's
all punk heart,
messily thudding."
—EILEEN MYLES

jenne
thornton

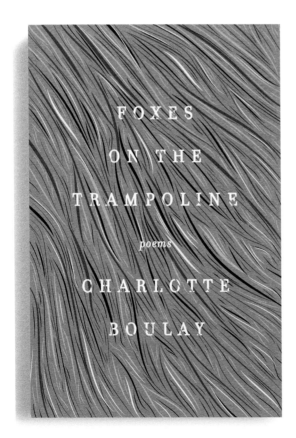

FOXES
ON THE
TRAMPOLINE

poems

CHARLOTTE
BOULAY

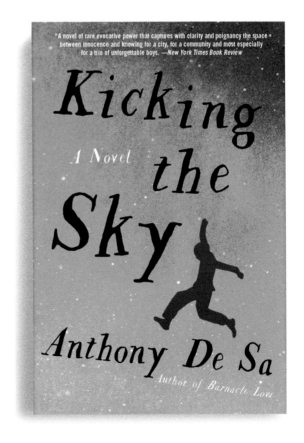

"A novel of rare evocative power that captures with clarity and poignancy the space
between innocence and knowing for a city, for a community and most especially
for a trio of unforgettable boys. —New York Times Book Review

Kicking
A Novel
the
Sky

Anthony De Sa
Author of Barnacle Love

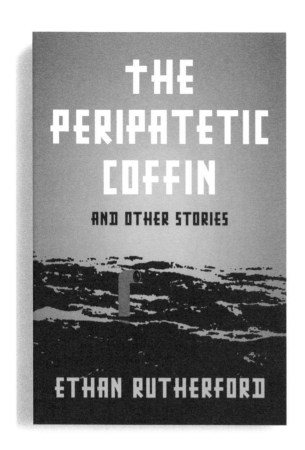

THE PERIPATETIC COFFIN

AND OTHER STORIES

ETHAN RUTHERFORD

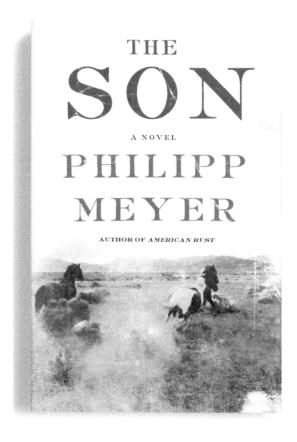

THE SON

A NOVEL

PHILIPP MEYER

AUTHOR OF *AMERICAN RUST*

THE TORTURE REPORT

WHAT THE DOCUMENTS SAY ABOUT AMERICA'S POST-9-11 TORTURE PROGRAM

LARRY SIEMS

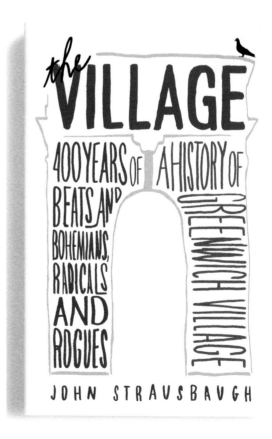

the VILLAGE

400 YEARS OF BEATS AND BOHEMIANS, RADICALS AND ROGUES

A HISTORY OF GREENWICH VILLAGE

JOHN STRAUSBAUGH

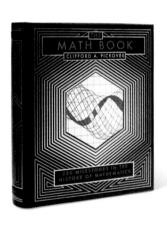

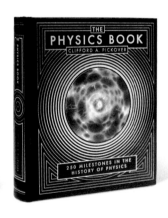

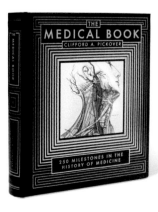

Steve Cooley

Steve Cooley operates Cooley Design Lab (CDL), a design studio founded in 2000 in New York City. Now located in South Portland, Maine, CDL specializes in book and music packaging. Prior to launching CDL, Steve was the creative director of Da Capo Press and Perseus Publishing, two imprints of the Perseus Books Group in Cambridge, Massachusetts. Before that, he was the founding art director for Houghton Mifflin's adult trade paperback imprint, Mariner Books, in Boston. He began his publishing career at Harcourt Brace Jovanovich in San Diego as a cover and jacket designer in the early 1990s. Steve has been privileged to work on titles from such authors as Italo Calvino, Carl Sandburg, Amos Oz, José Saramago, Arturo Pérez-Reverte, Octavio Paz, Anne Sexton, Mary Oliver, Charles Simic, Jhumpa Lahiri, Toby Young, Lawrence Block, Mickey Spillane, Michael Crichton, Richard Price, and Jonathan Lethem, among many others.

The Designer's Approach: When designing a book cover, I begin the process by learning as much as I can about the subject or story line (which is a common approach among designers). If it's a fiction title, then reading the manuscript is vital, but I don't feel that it's as important to read a complete manuscript when I'm working on certain nonfiction books. Depending on the topic and any initial impressions I may have, I start to think about whether I'll be using photography, illustration, or an all-type treatment.

Before I create any layouts, I typically go online and research other covers in the same genre or subject, in order to get a sense of what's already been done. I find that this especially comes in handy when working on historical nonfiction. For instance, if I'm assigned a book cover about a specific battle in WWII, and the publisher has requested a photograph, I would prefer to select one that hasn't already been used on a cover. Before the days of Amazon (and, frankly, the Internet as we know it), the only way to accomplish this reconnaissance was to visit bookstores and libraries regularly—which is still a good habit.

I then work up pencil sketches, but occasionally I will use the computer screen as my drawing board if an idea is nearly formed in my head. I also like to get information from the editor, if possible. Editors can supply crucial details about the text and, in a lot of cases, will have already heard suggestions from the author regarding potential cover thoughts. Sometimes an author's suggestions aren't objective enough, but this input can still be helpful.

At this stage I will experiment with color and typefaces, depending on the subject and whether I am using an image or just type. I may go through dozens of layouts that don't work before I arrive at a few good solutions, or I may solve the problem on the first or second try. Hopefully, the end result will be a cover that I'm pleased with, that satisfies the publisher and the author, and that makes an impact in the bookstore.

BEHIND
MY
EYES
LI-YOUNG LEE

poems

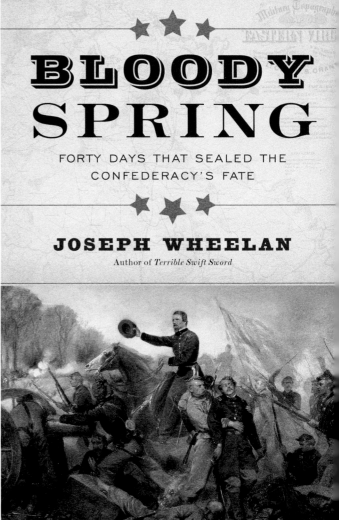

AMONG THE CREATIONISTS

Dispatches from the
Anti-Evolutionist Front Line

JASON ROSENHOUSE

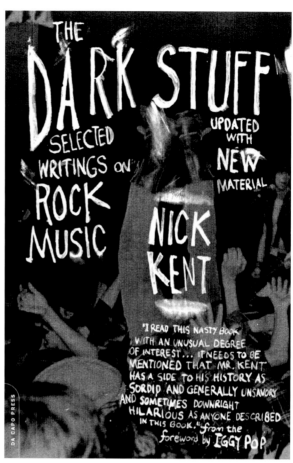

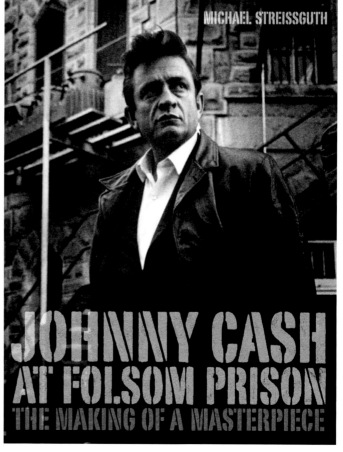

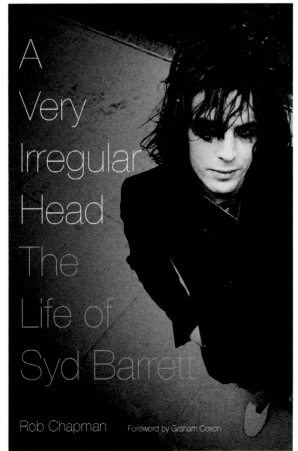

Strick&Williams

Claire Williams Martinez and Charlotte Strick joined forces in 2014 to form the graphic design agency Strick&Williams. This agency creates brand identities, books, environmental graphics, communication programs, and websites for nonprofits, publishing, academic, and art institutions. Clients include Abrams Books, Farrar, Straus and Giroux, W. W. Norton, *The Paris Review*, Weese Langley Weese Architects, and Columbia University.

Strick&Williams's Approach: For years we approached book jacket design, like most in the field, with a single perspective. When we joined forces in 2014 to form our studio, Strick&Williams, it became possible to share design viewpoints on each project. Each of us reads the manuscript, then we discuss it and compare notes, split up the research, and pass designs back and forth to one another. This makes for a really rich and supportive way of working. Between us, we have decades of work and experience in book publishing, and we still feel challenged and excited by each new title.

Pg 200, top left: Farrar, Straus, and Giroux / Farrar, Straus & Giroux Originals, Illustrator: Fernando Vicente, Art director: Rodrigo Corral; top right: Farrar, Straus, and Giroux, Art director: Rodrigo Corral; bottom left: W. W. Norton, Art director: Ingsu Liu; bottom right: Random House, Art director: Paolo Pepe I Pg 201, top left: Fig Tree Books, Illustrator: Ariana Nehmad Ross; top right: Fig Tree Books; bottom left: Jacket illustrations: (wildflowers) © Pingwin/Getty Images; (cannon) © Getty Images; (soldiers) © Andrew Chin, Shutterstock/GettyImages; bottom right: Abrams Books, Illustrator: Ariana Nehmad Ross, Art director: John Gall

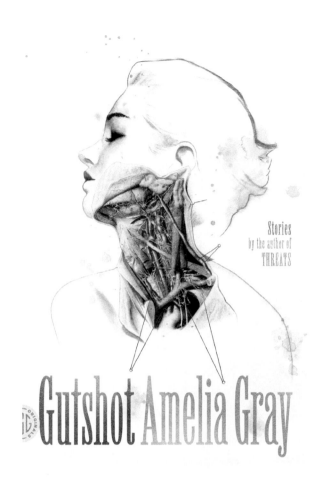

Stories
by the author of
THREATS

Gutshot Amelia Gray

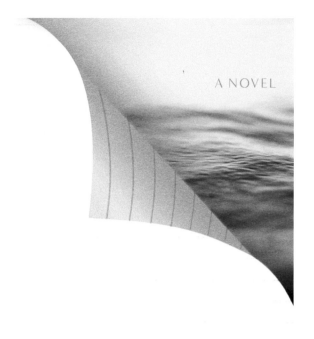

A NOVEL

OUTLINE
RACHEL CUSK

ORACLE

POEMS

CATE MARVIN

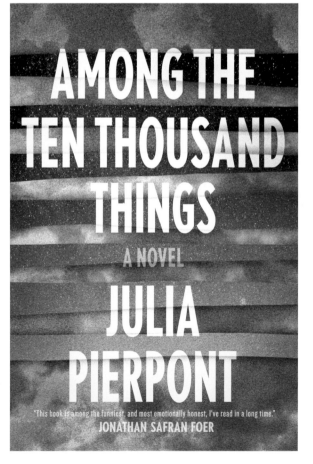

AMONG THE
TEN THOUSAND
THINGS
A NOVEL
JULIA
PIERPONT

"This book is among the funniest, and most emotionally honest, I've read in a long time."
JONATHAN SAFRAN FOER

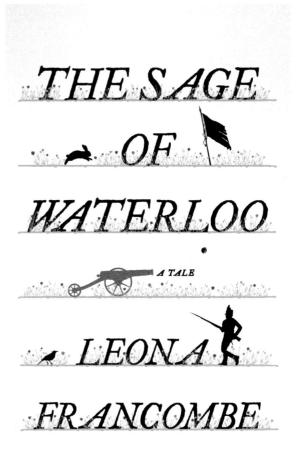

Tal Goretsky

Tal Goretsky is the art director of Broadway Books and Three Rivers Press at Penguin Random House. He was previously art director of Scribner, and worked as a senior designer at Penguin Press.

The Designer's Approach: I begin each project by reading the book or at least part of it. As I read, I see cover ideas in my head that I sketch and then try to execute. Usually, the images I see don't exist on stock photo sites, so I will have to illustrate them in Photoshop from multiple image sources and photograph objects I need. I often draw the type and digitally manipulate it.

Pg 203, left: Penguin, This was Tal Goretsky's first cover designed at Penguin. He photographed a coworker running on the roof of the publishing house. right: Penguin, Goretsky had to design this cover very quickly, so he only had a short time to read the beginning of the book. He knew right away it was a surreal story and that the main character rode a bicycle, so he put this image together. | Pg 204: Riverhead Books, Goretsky made the type out of sparkles and stencils | Pg 205, top left: Penguin; top right: Penguin, Goretsky designed the cover and then gave it to his tailor to sew the type, which was then photographed. bottom left: Penguin, Goretsky's intention was for this cover to look like a comic book. bottom right: Penguin, The designer wanted the title to evoke the ornate type of the medieval period, so he used alchemical symbols on the series design. | Pg 206: Hogarth, Goretsky wanted the helicopter wind and sand storm to blow away the type. | Pg 207, left: Gallery Books, Goretsky is a big fan of illustrator Sean Freeman, so he asked him to illustrate the cover and the smoky type. right: Random House, Goretsky had a lot of fun trying to sass up the type and create an atmospheric, ornate image.

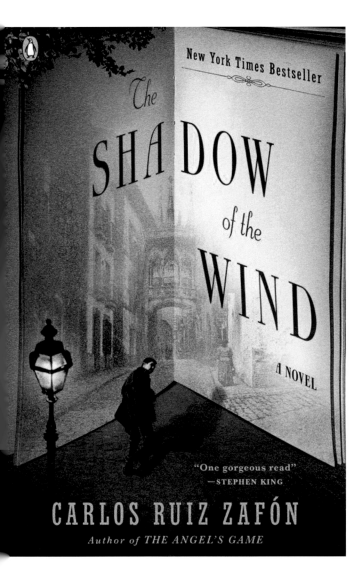

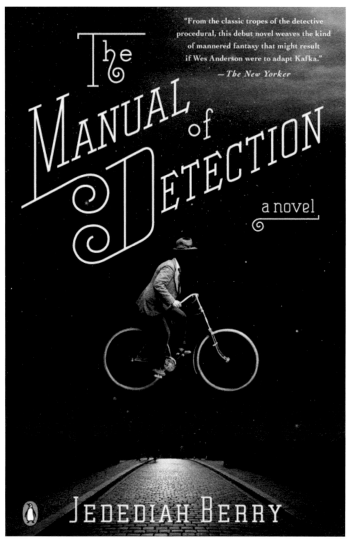

MY NAME IS MEMORY

a novel

ANN BRASHARES

New York Times Bestselling *Author of*
THE SISTERHOOD OF THE TRAVELING PANTS

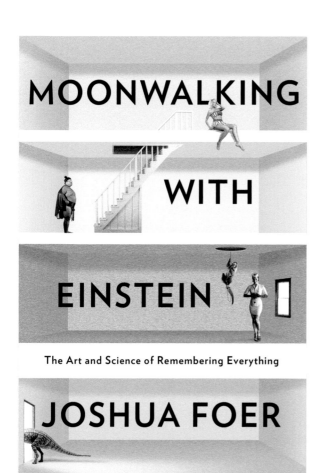

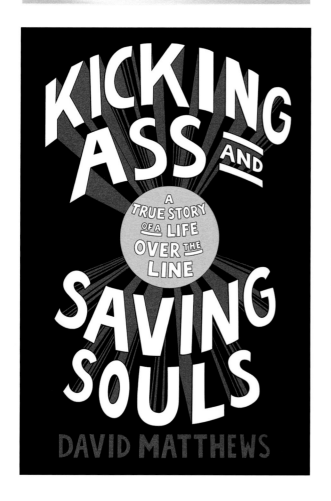

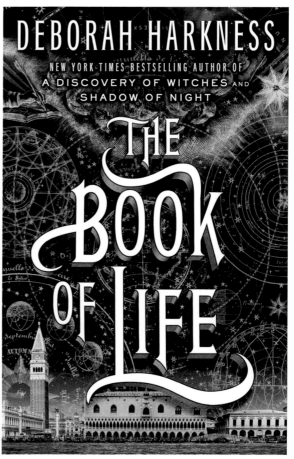

THE WATCH

A NOVEL

JOYDEEP ROY-BHATTACHARYA

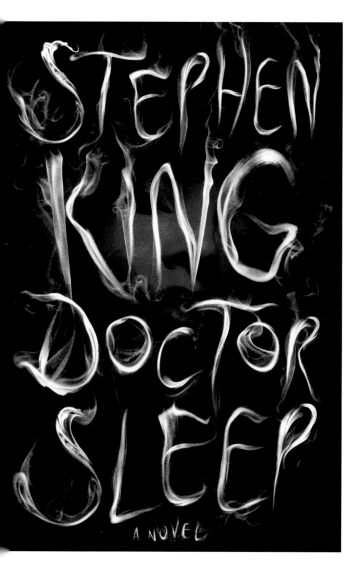

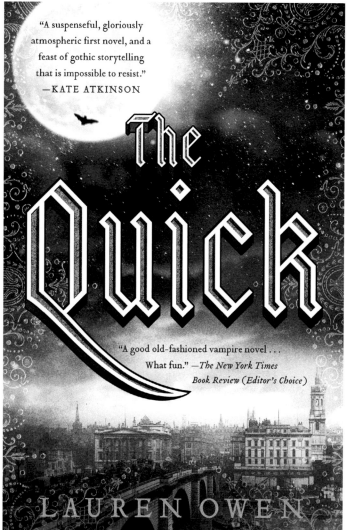

Thomas Ng

Thomas Ng is a graphic designer specializing in hand-lettering, book covers, and editorial illustration.

The Designer's Approach: *Thomas Ng's How to Design a Book Cover:* Get the Project > Have Goals + Sketch > Get It Done (Learn, Do it, or Hire Talent) > Kill It When It's Time > Share with Friends. Hold the best sketch, toss all the other sketches. Don't be afraid to turn down work. Make lots of versions (to not get hung up). Work big picture. Keep everyone excited, get it approved. Polish before the finish line. Don't work on projects that stress you out or all-consume your life with no visible results. Have a calling card. Work with others (photo researchers, other illustrators, Find and Seekers).

Pg 209, **left:** Oxford University Press; **right:** Spiegel & Grau | Pg 210, **top left:** unpublished design; **top right:** Spiegel&Grau; **bottom left:** Touchstone; **bottom right:** unpublished design | Pg 211, **left:** Simon & Schuster; **right:** Random House

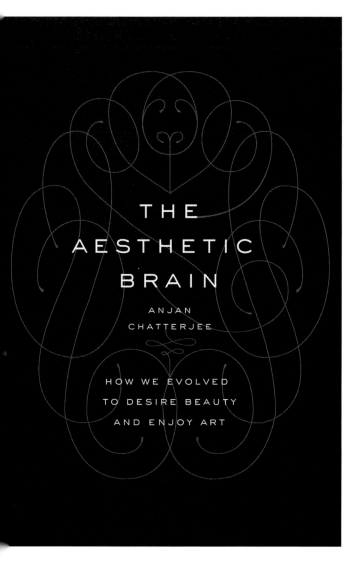

THE
AESTHETIC
BRAIN

ANJAN
CHATTERJEE

HOW WE EVOLVED
TO DESIRE BEAUTY
AND ENJOY ART

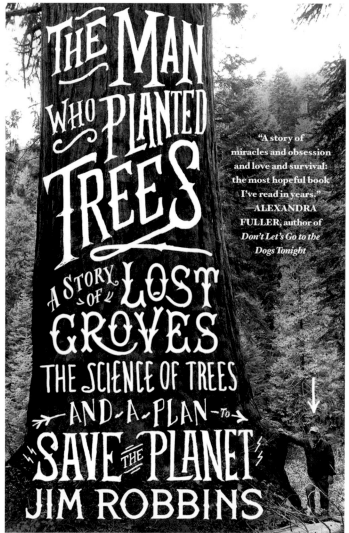

THE MAN
WHO PLANTED
TREES

"A story of
miracles and obsession
and love and survival:
the most hopeful book
I've read in years."
—ALEXANDRA
FULLER, author of
Don't Let's Go to the
Dogs Tonight

A STORY OF LOST
GROVES
THE SCIENCE OF TREES
AND A PLAN TO
SAVE THE PLANET
JIM ROBBINS

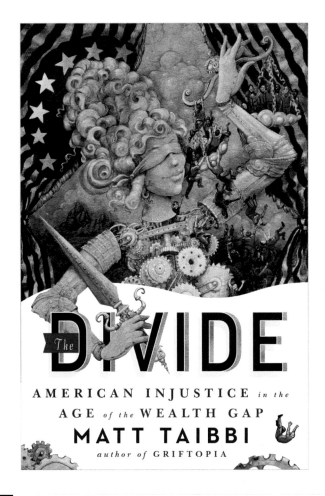

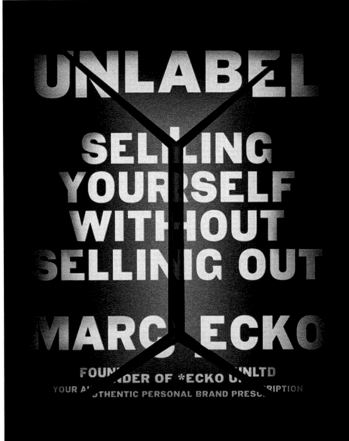

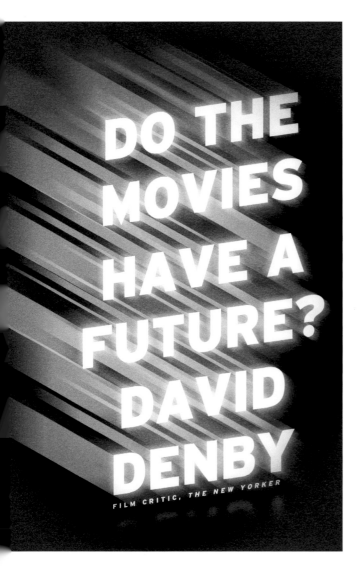

Tim Phelan

Tim Phelan is a designer living and working in London. His current skillset allows him to work across a broad spectrum of disciplines such as print, branding, and digital design. He tends to thrive more through variety as it allows him to constantly be honing and learning new skills across a number of constantly evolving areas. A good bit of problem solving and a space to do great work is all he needs. In Tim's spare time, he likes to write and illustrate for children's books. He's very curious as to how the form of the book is evolving, so keeping in touch with aspects of digital publishing provides him with a great wealth of inspiration and insight.

The Designer's Approach: Designing a book series is always a challenge. One of the main challenges is to define a unique concept for each book while creating certain consistencies in the overall series. I always love the challenge of condensing complex information into designs that communicate underlying themes of a story. Having not read H. G. Wells before, I had a lot of reading to do. With this series, I wanted to move away from the computer and try something more organic that would also allow for unexpected results and interesting experimentation. I arrived at the sole use of paper and collage; I've always believed that giving yourself rules and limitations can give way to the best results.

For *The Invisible Man*, I used torn paper to mimic a straight jacket, it struck me that I could further use this device to emphasize the characters' underlying insanity. With *The War of the Worlds*, I drew inspiration from the Orson Welles radio adaptation that panicked America in 1938. As extracts of the novel are written in a formal journalistic style; my starting point referenced torn newspapers and half-tone patterns. For *The Time Machine*, I drew inspiration from blueprints, diagrams, scribbled thoughts, and lots of math. Although *The Island of Dr Moreau* contains a lot of social allegories, it's essentially the tale of a mad scientist who dissects and turns people into animals. This was the hardest concept to define. Initially, I was experimenting with dirt and muddy fingerprints. Eventually, I whittled it down to a simpler metaphor: a doctor's stethoscope/dog lead.

The back of each jacket contains a specific quote from every novel that should engage a potential reader. As these novels are such classics, I felt it was redundant to have the synopsis on the back. Instead, a "Did You Know?" fact can be found on each book that gives the reader a unique fact about how books have had such an important influence on science fiction and popular culture. Furthermore, to push the function and form of the book jacket, I introduced a tear-away bookmark that could be used by the reader.

Pg 213, all covers: Spine Publishing I Pg 214, left: Unpublished; right: Self-published

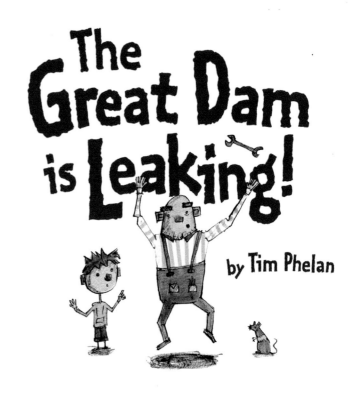

Timothy Goodman

Timothy Goodman is a designer, illustrator, and an art director based in New York City. Currently, he runs his own studio, working for clients such as Airbnb, Google, J. Crew, Nike, *The New Yorker*, and *The New York Times*. Previously, Timothy worked in-house at Apple Inc., where he helped integrate Apple's visual language across third party environments, retail stores, and campaign launches. Prior to that, he worked for the experiential design firm Collins. He has received awards from most major design and illustration publications, including the ADC *Young Guns*, *GDUSA*'s "People To Watch" and *Print* magazine's "New Visual Artist." Timothy began his career as a book jacket designer for Simon & Schuster, and he graduated from the School of Visual Arts, where he now teaches. In 2013, Timothy and Jessica Walsh created a personal project called "40 Days of Dating." Recently, they sold the film rights of their story to Warner Bros., and they wrote a book about their experience for Abrams.

The Designer's Approach: My process is always different, but it has definitely evolved over the last eight years since I graduated. In the beginning, I would send in three or four "finished" cover sketches. I would slave over these. Now, I do very quick marker sketches—with notes of how I'd execute—to show the idea first. Then we pick one and I execute it. It's a much more efficient process.

Pg 216: unpublished design created for Scribner | Pg 217, top left: Picador; top right: Scribner; bottom left: Farrar, Straus & Giroux; bottom right: unpublished cover design for W. W. Norton

SILVER SCREEN FIEND

LEARNING ABOUT LIFE FROM AN ADDICTION TO FILM

PATTON OSWALT

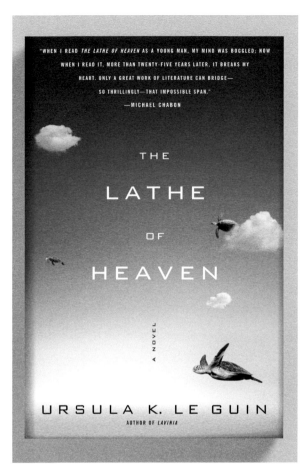

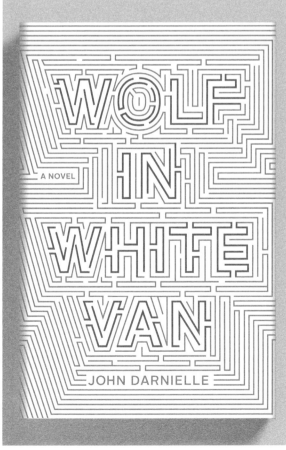

Will Staehle

Will Staehle grew up reading comics and working summers at his parent's design firm in Wisconsin. He was art director for HarperCollins Publishers in New York, and the design director at JibJab in Los Angeles. Will was labeled by *Print* magazine as one of the "Top 20 Under 30 New Visual Artists," an ADC Young Gun, and has exhibited a solo show of work at the Type Director's Club. His work has appeared in various design annuals, as well as in the AIGA's "50 books/50 covers exhibit." Will now resides in sunny Seattle where he runs his own studio using his design and illustration background to create book jackets, stylized posters, and odd comics to ensure that he gets as little sleep as possible.

The Designer's Approach: I think my process is quite standard, but here we go. First and foremost I'll receive reading materials for new cover projects. Generally, this is the full book, but sometimes it's only a synopsis and a few chapters (since we often begin the cover process very early).

I read through the material, making little rough thumbnails of various ideas throughout. And, at the end, I'll circle back and weed out anything that doesn't quite feel right. Sometimes, I'll scan in a few of the thumbnails for a base to work off of, and other times I'll just start directly on the computer while referencing the thumbnail sketches. As I start working digitally, many of these ideas start to solidify and oftentimes change into something else that I didn't expect entirely. I end up executing a handful of concepts, export out a PDF, and pray to the art director gods that they like something!

Pg 219: Twelve | Pg 220, top left: Tor Books; top right: Grand Central Publishing; bottom left: Tor Books; bottom right: Harper Design | Pg 221: Harper Perennial | Pg 222, top left: Harper Perennial; top right: Twelve; bottom: Harper Perennial

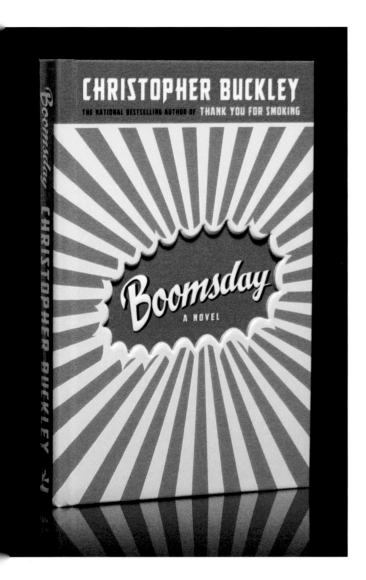

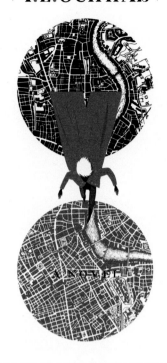

"EPIC AND GRIPPING." **V.E.SCHWAB** —PUBLISHERS WEEKLY, STARRED REVIEW, ON *VICIOUS*

A NOVEL

ADARKERSHADEOFMAGIC

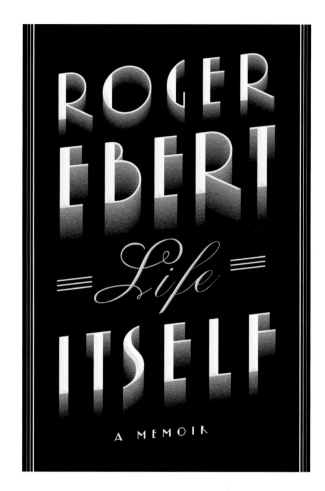

ROGER EBERT

Life

ITSELF

A MEMOIR

the REVOLUTIONS

LONDON, ENGLAND   A NOVEL   EIGHTEEN-NINETY

ESSAGE
SPIRIT
ORLD

rs after Truth are
y invited to a celebrated
evening by the celebrated
medium Mrs. Emma
London for one week only!
t the spirits "have in store
prehend the meaning of
zzling events! Pierce the
of the heavenly spheres!
udents only. "Skeptics"
onations encouraged.

RM OF THE
NTURY

veiled a fearful scene of
n such as no Londoner
mbers, save perhaps
have suffered a tropical
Men of science say such
re unheard-of in these
fet this morning scarcely
e or chimney in all of
ands upright.

FIG. 3

FIR
RAVAGE
DEPTF

There has been a fire on
Street. It could be se
night up and down the
bright and dreadful as
star Wormwood. Wh
once a street of wareho
in ruins. The police
themselves mystified.
[so say those unlucky so
were there that night]

"REPRESENTS EVERYTHING GREAT SCIENCE FICTION SHOULD ASPIRE TO."—THE CLEVELAND PLAIN DEALER ON *THE HALF-MADE WORLD*

FELIX GILMAN

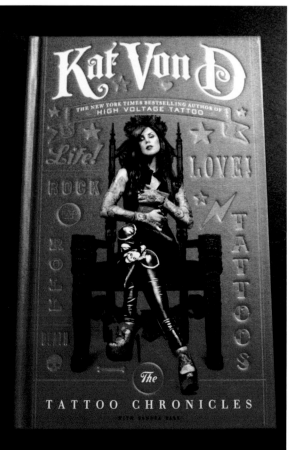

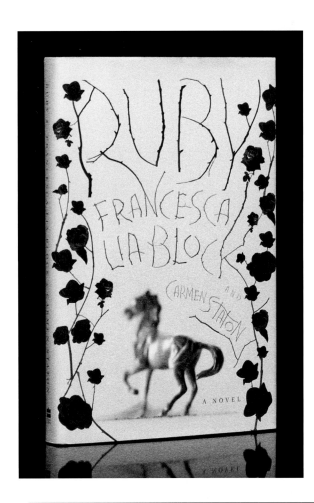

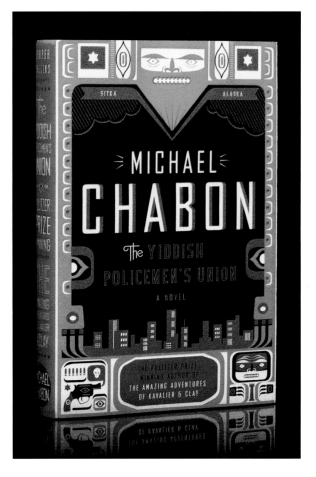

DESIGNER CONTACT INFORMATION

Adam Johnson
cmykadam.com
cmyk.adam@gmail.com

Adly Elewa
Adlyelewa.com
Adly.m.elewa@gmail.com

Alex Merto
alexmerto@gmail.com

Alex Camlin
alexcamlin.com
alexander.camlin@gmail.com

Bill Jones
bjones1764@optimum.net

Catherine Casalino
www.catherinecasalino.com
catherinecasalino@gmail.com

Charlotte Strick
hi@charlottestrick.com

Chelsea Hunter
chelsea@seehunters.com
www.seehunters.com

Christopher Moisan
christophermoisandesign.tumblr.com
chrmoisan@gmail.com

Christopher Sergio
www.csergiodesign.com
csergiodesign@gmail.com

Connie Gabbert
www.conniegabbertdesign.com
connie@thesparebutton.com

Crush Creative
www.crushed.co.uk
contact@crushed.co.uk

David Drummond
david@salamanderhill.com
www.salamanderhill.com
www.daviddrummond.blogspot.ca

David Gee
davidgeebookdesign@gmail.com

David High
highdzn@earthlink.net
www.ralphdelpozzo.com
www.highdzn.com

Emily Mahon
www.emilymahon.com

Ferran López
www.ferranlopez.com
elotrolopez@yahoo.es

Fort
iwantto@visitfort.com
visitfort.com

Helen Yentus
www.helenyentus.com

Isaac Tobin
www.isaactobin.com
isaac@isaactobin.com

Jacob Covey
www.unflown.com
covey@unflown.com

Jamie Keenan
www.keenandesign.com
keenan@keenandesign.com

Jarrod A. Taylor
jarrod.a.taylor@gmail.com

Jason Booher
jasonbooher.com
jbooher@penguinrandomhouse.com

Jason Heuer
www.jasonheuer.com
jason@jasonheuer.com

Jason Ramirez
www.jasonramirez.net
www.behance.net/jasonramirez
twitter.com/jasonramirez

Jennifer Heuer
www.jenniferheuer.com

Jenny Carrow
www.jennifercarrow.com
jennycarrow@gmail.com

Jim Tierney
jim@jimtierneyart.com

Kimberly Glyder
www.kimberlyglyder.com
kglyder@kimberlyglyder.com

Kirk DouPonce
www.DogEaredDesign.com
kirk@dogeareddesign.com

Mark Melnick
www.markmelnick.com
tomelnick@earthlink.net

Matt Avery
www.mattaverydesign.com

Matt Dorfman
www.metalmother.com
matt.dorfman@gmail.com

Melissa Gerber
melissagerberdesign@gmail.com
www.creativehotlist.com/mgerber2

Michael Kellner
www.kellnerbookdesign.com

Natalie Olsen
www.kisscutdesign.com
info@kisscutdesign.com
twitter: @KisscutDesign

Natalie F. Smith
www.nataliefsmith.com
nataliefsmith@me.com

Nathan Burton
www.nathanburtondesign.com

Nicole Caputo
nicole@nicolecaputo.com
www.nicolecaputo.com
https://www.behance.net/
NicoleCaputo

Oliver Munday
www.olivermunday.com
www.omunday.tumblr.com

Paul Buckley
www.paulbuckleydesign.com
pbuckley@penguinrandomhouse.com

Rex Bonomelli
rexbonomelli.com
rbonomelli@mac.com

Steve Attardo
NINETYNORTH Design
steve@ninetynorthdesign.com
www.ninetynorthdesign.com

Steve Cooley
www.cooleydesignlab.com
www.designerdroppings.com
steve@cooleydesignlab.com

Strick&Williams
hi@strickandwilliams.com

Tal Goretsky
talgoretsky@gmail.com

Thomas Ng
www.thomasng.org
studio@thomasng.org

Tim Phelan
www.timwitted.com
tim@timphelan.net
twitter: @tim_phelan

Tim Goodman
www.tgoodman.com
timothy@tgoodman.com

Will Staehle
www.unusualco.com